# FORGIVENESS!

## THE KEY TO
# EMOTIONAL FREEDOM

## THE POWER OF LETTING GO

Graeme and Julia Cann

Forgiveness/The Key to Emotional Freedom © Copyright: Graeme & Julia Cann, 2025

All rights reserved. No part of this publication may be reproduced, stored in a retrieval system or transmitted in any form by any means, electronic, mechanical, photocopying, recording or otherwise, without the prior permission of the author — except in the case of brief quotation embodied in critical review and certain other non-commercial uses permitted by copyright law.

Cover picture source by G. Lewis. Used with permission.

Forgiveness! The Key to Emotional Freedom: The Power of Letting Go

1. Forgiveness.  2. Emotional Healing.  I. Title.

ISBN: 978-1-76411-170-6

All scripture references (unless specified) from the New Living Translation (NLT) © 2004, 2007, 2013, 2015. Used with permission.

PUBLISHED BY GRAEME CANN

www.graemecann.com

# TABLE of CONTENTS

Foreword ............................................. IV
Acknowledgements................................VI
Introduction......................................... VIII
Chapter One         *Collateral Damage*..............12
Chapter Two         *Woundedness* ...................24
Chapter Three       *Only Way Forward* ............34
Chapter Four        *Wounds and Scars*............. 44
Chapter Five        *When it is Time*.................50
Chapter Six         *Prepare Yourself*................60
Chapter Seven       *Broken Saw*..................... 68
Chapter Eight       *FAQ's*........................74
Chapter Nine        *Three Things*....................82
Chapter Ten         *Before You Say* ................ 92
Chapter Eleven      *How to Turn the Key*........... 100
Chapter Twelve      *Be-Attitudes of Forgiveness*......114
Chapter Thirteen    *Pay Up ... or Else*.............122
Chapter Fourteen    *The Final Word*................134

# FOREWORD

Pain is part of the human condition, and experiencing pain from others, sadly, happens all too often. To assert that internalised pain can only be resolved by forgiving the one who caused the pain, raises numerous difficult issues, many of which are addressed in this book. Using deeply impacting stories, theologically balanced comments, scripturally sound insights and practical keys, Graeme and Julia Cann present a way forward for those who are living in their self-made prison of resentment.

'Forgiveness! The Key to Emotional Freedom' addresses the reasons why we should forgive, the importance of knowing when to forgive, the way to prepare ourselves to forgive and finally the five steps of forgiveness. The authors' responses to the seven frequently asked questions about forgiveness are helpful and insightful coming from more than sixty years of ministering to people who are seeking to break free.

I warmly recommend this book. The teaching is so practical, and the process of forgiving presented with such clarity. It is an essential read for every person — especially those who struggle with resentment and bitterness, and who need to know the 'why', 'when' and 'how' of forgiveness. I also recommend this book as a helpful resource for those who are people helpers — in their ministry of counselling and pastoring.

Having read *'Forgiveness! The Key to Emotional Healing: The Power of Letting Go'*, I plan to read it again and again! And in doing so, I pray for the courage to continue living out the principles this book presents — in my own daily life.

May God bless you as you read this book ... and as you share it with others. And may He continue to bless and strengthen Graeme and Julia, as they minister to others — not only out of the deep well of their own personal experience, but also their deep love for the God who heals.

Rev. Dr Brian Birkett MACMN, MACSA, MAAOS, AMACCA
Director, Springboard Consulting
Director, Healthy Pastors.com.au

# ACKNOWLEDGEMENTS

For a very long time Julia and I have been concerned that books written about forgiveness and sermons preached on the same important subject have always told us what forgiveness means and why we should forgive but rarely ... how we *should* forgive.

Our prayer is that "FORGIVENESS: THE KEY TO EMOTIONAL HEALING," will confirm all the good and helpful things that have been said and written about the 'Why' and the 'When' of forgiveness — while at the same time presenting a very clear pathway for those seeking the 'How.'

While we recognise that it is God who gives us the power to live fully and freely through His unlimited love and forgiveness of us, we also know from our study of God's Word — especially after more than sixty years of ministry to Christians and non-Christians — that there is no freedom unless we obey God's command to love and forgive others as He has loved and forgiven us. It is in this act of obedience that we discover there are mindsets, attitudes and processes that assist us.

We want to thank all those who have contributed in many ways to make the desire to produce this book become a reality. To Colin, Alex and Claire who have added their stories to ours, and the many fellow travellers who have enriched our lives by allowing us to share their journey.

We also thank Vision Christian Media for permission to include their report of the 2022 National Prayer Breakfast. This report written by Tony Davenport, covered the address given by Danny and Leila Abdallah.

As always, we want to acknowledge our family from whom we receive so much love and encouragement. Our children, our grandchildren and our great grandchildren are a constant source of joy and encouragement to us.

Finally, we thank our heavenly Father from whom we receive the truth and grace we have sought to share with you in this book.

# INTRODUCTION

In a world where pain and hurt are inevitable, forgiveness emerges as a beacon of hope and emotional liberation. Forgiveness is not about excusing or condoning the actions that caused us harm; rather, it is about freeing ourselves from the shackles of bitterness and resentment that weigh heavily on our hearts. It is an active choice, a powerful tool that empowers us to reclaim our peace and happiness.

Many of us believe that forgiveness is conditional, dependent on the remorse and apology of the offender. This traditional model places the power in the hands of the perpetrator, leaving the victim in a state of helplessness.

However, true forgiveness transcends this limitation, offering us the opportunity to take control of our own healing process. By embracing forgiveness, we set ourselves free from the emotional imprisonment that hinders our growth and wellbeing. We release the need for revenge and retribution, understanding that no amount of punishment can erase the pain we have endured. Forgiveness allows us to break the cycle of hurt and anger, creating space for love, joy, and inner peace to flourish.

Whenever we have opportunity to speak or write about forgiveness, we are fully aware that to many listeners or readers, the assumption that they would ever forgive their hurter is offensive. The very suggestion may even feel abusive to some. We understand that. We have been there. Many of you who are starting to read this book have been there too.

The idea of forgiving a drunk driver for causing the death of a child, a family member for breaching trust, or an individual for abuse, can be very challenging. Forgiving a person when the damage they caused continues to negatively impact our lives is also unthinkable.

You do not have to agree of course, but we think that the reason it is unthinkable to many is because they do not understand what forgiveness is.

For a long time, the world has been taught that 'if someone has wronged another, they should apologise and if the person they have wronged thinks they are appropriately remorseful, they should accept the apology and pardon them and that constitutes forgiveness.

Does that sound fair? Or just? Most people who have been hurt by others may find this model of forgiveness ineffective, even inappropriate.

In this book we are attempting to present another understanding of and process towards forgiveness. Both the Hebrew word 'Salach' and the Greek word 'Aphiemi' mean 'to set loose,' and are translated as 'forgive' in the English Bible. This implies that holding onto resentment and bitterness traps us in a web of emotional pain.

## to be free ...
## we need to 'set ourselves loose'.

This Biblical model suggests that freedom from our emotional prison is only possible when we choose to forgive the hurter for the wrong's they have committed against us. Hence the chief beneficiary of forgiveness is the forgiver, not the one forgiven.

Bitterness and resentment are revenge based. It is the hurt person demanding revenge. Needing to 'get even,' but rarely able to because no punishment that we could devise and legally impose, could ever atone for the hurt, the humiliation, the grief and the emotional or physical woundedness they have caused us.

We forgive another when we set them free from the obligation to suffer, at our hands, for what they have done to us. We are most likely to do this when we realise that being the victim, the judge and the hangman is costing us too much.

It is impossible to over-emphasise the high cost of living in a prison of resentment — it drains every ounce of energy from us.

As the 'victim', we are demanding justice but there is none given. As 'the judge', no sentence we impose will be enough. As the 'hangman', we face the reality that even a hanging will not take away our pain.

So, we live believing that nothing will ever change. Out of fear of being hurt again, we build walls or retreat into our private pain. The very worst aspect of living in this prison, is that we are not the only ones who are suffering. Our negative behaviours and reactions, triggered by wounds and memories, continue to be sources of pain. Hurting people become the 'hurters', and a new generation of people, living in their private prisons, begin their own experience of living angry and resentful lives.

Anxieties hinder us when we think about forgiving those who hurt us. We want to escape our prison of anger and resentment but at what cost? Surely our hurter does not deserve our forgiveness! It is unjust and unfair that we should be asked to do so.

It does not have to be like this. We do not need to wait for the hurter to apologise, and even if they did, it would appear so trite compared to what we have suffered. There is a better way.

**Don't wait any longer. Forgive!**

## Chapter One

# Collateral Damage

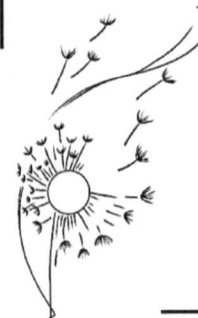

## *The first answer to the question: why forgive? ... because resentment damages us.*

It was the first of February 2020, when seven children happily walked together toward an ice cream shop in Sydney, Australia. A car driven by a drug and alcohol affected driver and travelling at 150kms per hour, mounted the footpath and struck them all. Antony Abdallah and his two sisters Selina and Angelina, and their cousin Veronique died that day. In 2022, their parents were the guest speakers at the National Prayer Breakfast in Canberra.

The following excerpts are from an article by Tony Davenport published by Vision Christian Media in 2023.

> *'A Christian couple, Danny and Leila Abdallah, touched hearts across the country, when they almost immediately forgave the driver, who had killed their of three children and their niece. Guests at the 2022 National Prayer Breakfast erupted in applause when Danny revealed that the driver, Samuel Davidson, has become a Christian in prison, where he is reading his bible daily and talking to other prisoners about His faith in Christ.*
>
> *Danny said, "On the day of the accident, I was faced with a question. A question no father should ever be asked to answer. What are you going to*

do? You can lose all your family either by seeking revenge and remaining bitter. Or you can forgive and lose half your family. What a tough question! Today I want to talk to you about the fruits of forgiveness. I forgave the driver who killed our children and Veronique. And the reason I forgave him was I wanted to be obedient to our Lord and Saviour and honour him whatever the cost."

After hearing that Samuel Davidson had decided to follow Jesus, Danny tells us what happened next. *"I asked Samuel Davidson, why? He said, 'Because I want what you have. Your act of forgiveness is the reason why I wanted to unite myself with Jesus.'*

*"I was blown away!*

*"Some of you here might say. Why would you forgive him? He doesn't deserve it. And maybe so. But I deserve peace. And my wife and kids deserve peace as well.*

*"Sometimes, you don't realise that to carry an unforgiving heart becomes a burden on the ones you love the most. Holding a grudge, refusing to forgive, and remaining bitter is contagious. You can quite easily pass it on to your loved ones. Understand that being bitter and unforgiving can disconnect you from the ones you love the most, and more importantly, disconnect you from God.*

> *"Today, I want to encourage you all to forgive. To honour our Creator, as I did. And I promise you, with perseverance and patience you will see the fruits of forgiveness in your home, workplace, community and our beautiful nation."* '

Leila explains what she did shortly after the accident.

> ' *"I went back to the scene of the tragedy, and I knelt upright, at each of the places each child had lain. I prayed The Lord's Prayer seven times. Once for each child. The Lord's Prayer, which is the most powerful prayer, says 'Forgive us our trespasses as we forgive those who trespass against us'. The more I prayed it and the more I walked on the scene, the heavier I felt. I felt that I was walking the stations of the cross. And I saw Jesus on the cross. And I heard Him saying, 'Father, forgive them, for they do not know what they are doing.' "* '

Leila continues:

> ' *"Forgiveness is the core message of Christianity. Forgiveness is the greatest gift you can give to yourself and to others. It will set you free from anger and bitterness. It brings you hope and peace. And in our case, it is bringing us new life and the freedom to dream again. I still look at life with eyes of empathy and compassion. Life is still beautiful. People around us are still amazing. We did not*

*allow the accident to ruin our life, or to take away more than it took from us. Forgiveness is liberating. It gives you resilience. Forgiveness started in our hearts, and it has become a movement and a National Day of Forgiveness, because the world needs forgiveness. Everyone needs forgiveness. Every day, I am challenged to forgive." '*

At this point, you may be wondering why we need another book on forgiveness?

We have three reasons for writing this book. To explore 'WHY' ... freedom from hurt and resentment is important. 'WHEN' ... we know that forgiveness should be offered and 'HOW' ... to navigate the sometimes difficult pathway to true forgiveness. Our hope is that you will have the same three reasons for reading it.

We are '*experts*' on resentment. In fact, we are just two of millions of experts. Not because any of us have studied it or written a thesis on it, but because we have all practised it, or in numerous cases, are still perfecting the art of being resentful.

Julia writes: "*For Graeme, it began with a painful event in his childhood and was directed at a person he should have been able to respect and admire. Instead, as a little boy, he first felt confused by the events, then the confusion became fear and in time the fear became anger. And because anger is an ugly and unacceptable emotion, he internalised it and although he did not anticipate it, it became his master.*

"His is a familiar story, except that resentment does not always begin in childhood, nor is it always directed at just one person but numerous people, for multiple reasons. For many years, us 'experts' believed that our confusion, fear and resentment were justifiable emotions and were not damaging or destructive. We saw them as appropriate reactions to mistreatment and harm. But we were wrong!

"The stark truth is that when we normalise and internalise these negative emotional responses, our spirits are damaged, and we begin to see ourselves and our world through the spectacles of resentment. Speaking from personal experience, Graeme recalls that from his childhood into his adulthood, a multitude of triggers preceded outbursts of anger, many of which attracted reproval and discipline from others, which left him with feelings that ranged from outrage to shame.

"At the age of seventeen, he had a deeply spiritual experience that significantly changed his life. He realized for the first time that his heavenly Father, God, and his own family loved and forgave him despite his unacceptable behaviours. The downside of what was otherwise a transformational experience, however, was that rather than deal with his resentment, he buried it even deeper than before. It would be more than twenty-five years before he would commence the journey that would bring him freedom.

"We married at 21 years of age, and we were very happy. We loved each other and the ministry we were engaged in, and we were thankful for the four children born to us in the first seven years of our marriage. The shadow that hung over our *marriage, was that from time to time, Graeme would suddenly become angry and on other occasions extremely sad. I was confused and hurt by these actions. Graeme also felt confused and embarrassed."*

Whilst Julia had shared her childhood experiences which included the death of her father, when she was only thirteen years of age, and her health struggles as a child and a teenager, Graeme had never shared his childhood experiences with her, but by burying both the painful memories and the negative emotions, mistakenly believed that they were dealt with.

Graeme tells the next part of his story:

*"In 1978 we had the opportunity of attending a course for Pastors at The Narramore Foundation in Los Angeles. As part of the course, we had to book a counselling session with a psychologist. For the very first time I told my story to someone who really seemed to care. I was amazed and shocked by the depth of the emotion I felt. When I had finished sharing, the counsellor allowed me to sit for a time as I sobbed out years of pain."*

*"When at last he spoke, he helped me understand what had just happened. The outpouring of emotion that day, came from the very same place that the anger and sorrow had been coming from for many years. The difference, however, was that back then it had been the emotional dysfunction that resulted from internalising the confusion, fear and anger that I had*

*experienced as a child; but now, it was the release of many years of buried pain.*

*"I would like to say that at that moment I was completely free. But that would not be the truth. The truth is that although I experienced the relief that came from knowing that I could tell my story, and that people would understand, and not condemn me, and that I was not responsible for my abuse, and that my shame belonged to another — anger toward the perpetrator — rose like bile in my mouth. Then, once again, my counsellor listened intently and patiently, until I finished spewing out my rage.*

*"I was still feeling intensely angry, when the counsellor spoke quietly and said that he would like me to consider two questions. The first question was, "Do you believe Jesus has suffered and died for every wrong you and the people you love have ever committed, and will ever commit in the future?" I told him that I did. I was a pastor and preacher, and every aspect of my ministry was based on that truth. He then said, "Good. My second question is, "Do you believe Jesus has died for every wrong committed against you by your abuser?" I was stunned by the question and initially refused to answer. I told him it was a trick question and did not deserve my consideration. He continued to push me to give him an answer.*

*"My problem was if I said that I did not believe that Jesus had paid the price for every sin committed*

against me, it made nonsense of my answer to the first question. If Jesus had paid the price for my sin, then he had undoubtedly paid the price for everybody's sin ... regardless of who they had sinned against.

"If on the other hand I answered the second question in the affirmative, it meant that my years of demanding, by my attitude and behaviour, that my perpetrator pay for what she had done to me, was pointless, as the price had already been paid two thousand years ago.

"In further sessions with the psychologist, I realised that if, through the death and resurrection of Jesus Christ, God's forgiveness was available to the person who had abused me, it was eminently possible for me to forgive her and experience both freedom from resentment and the capacity to move on from the impact of such a painful event.

"As wonderful as the actual act of forgiving my perpetrator was, the understanding that I had discovered a whole new freedom in my daily life, was even more so. This freedom originated from the truth — that the alternative to forgiving others is to remain resentful — and that this will always continue to damage us emotionally, mentally and relationally."

The Abdallah family story and Graeme's story differ in several significant ways. Danny and Leila, deeply wounded by the grief of losing three of their children, chose almost immediately to forgive the man who was responsible for their death. Their grief was complex.

Danny felt guilty because he had encouraged the children to visit the shop. The pain of losing their children in such a violent way was unbearable, and then there was the anger they felt toward the driver. The grief would in one sense define them forever, but choosing to forgive themselves and the driver, meant they were free to grieve as bereaved parents and at the same time grow as godly examples to their remaining children.

Graeme, on the other hand, chose not to forgive, and the consequence was that he would be defined, not by the abuse, but by his anger and resentment, hurting Julia and many others in the process, not because he had been abused, but because he refused to forgive. His experience, when he finally forgave his abuser, was that he was also able to grow through his journey, and like Danny and Leila, has dedicated his life to sharing the importance of forgiveness with others.

# FOR FURTHER REFLECTION

#1. Consider the Abdallah family's story of forgiveness. Have you ever asked yourself the question Danny asked himself. *"Do I remain bitter and resentful and risk losing everything and everyone that is important to me? Or do I forgive and move on in order to live a fulfilling life?"* Is it a question you should ask yourself?

#2. *'Forgiveness is sometimes difficult but essential if we are to find the key to emotional freedom.'* Are you able to embrace this statement? If you are refusing to forgive a person in your life, do you understand why?

#3. *'Internalising painful emotions has the potential to damage our mental, physical and relational health'.* Have you experienced this yourself ... or have you seen others experiencing it?

Chapter Two

# Woundedness

Our prayer in writing this book is that readers will come to recognise that the path to healing — through understanding and resolving internalised anger and resentment — begins with acknowledging three common forms of woundedness.

# #1. WOUNDEDNESS ... CAUSED BY A PERPETRATOR OR SIGNIFICANT OTHER.

Alina's story:

*"I was born in a rural town, the only child of my parents, Bob and Nancy. The town we lived in boasted a population of five hundred people and my father owned and worked a farm about 10kms north of where we lived. I loved the farm and its animals, spending hours there before I started school. My father encouraged me to believe that I could achieve anything I set my mind to, whereas my mother held quite a different perspective. It seemed that nothing I did pleased her. She constantly criticised me and my father.*

*"Her style of discipline was harsh ... even brutal. I was frequently beaten, refused food for hours and isolated in my room. When I was seven years of age, my father moved out to live on the farm. My mother refused to go with him, and I could visit my father every other weekend. To say that I lived for those weekends was an understatement.*

*"By the time I reached my early teens, mother's constant criticisms had taken their toll on me. At home, I retreated into*

a sullen silence, and at school every word of correction I received, triggered an angry reaction. My only companions were those, who like me, were rebellious and difficult. About this time my mother took her own life whilst a patient in a psychiatric hospital.

"My father's new partner made it clear to both of us, that I was not welcome to live with them on the farm. I not only felt abandoned, rejected and alone — but I felt guilty and ashamed. Remarkably, I convinced myself that if my mother, father and stepmother as adults who supposedly loved me, hurt me the way they did; then there must have been something radically wrong with me that deserved the treatment I had received from them.

"My later teenage years were a blur of alcohol-fuelled parties and illicit drug taking. When for the umpteenth time I hit a low spot in my life, I finally agreed to live with my aunt. A dedicated Christian, she had always been loving and generous toward me. She helped me find employment and encouraged me to attend Alcoholic Anonymous meetings. Gradually I got my life together. In my early twenties I fell in love with and married a loving man, and together we now have two children.

"I must admit, however, that although I love my husband very much, I frequently fly into rages if I ever feel criticised by him. I am currently undergoing therapy, which is providing valuable insights. For the first time, I am recognizing that my mother's and father's actions and my responses to those events have significantly impacted me."

There is a great deal to learn from Alina's story. Her mother's abusive behaviour and her father's rejection of her in favour of his new partner, were destructive behaviours for which they were responsible. Alina concluded, however, that she have deserved such treatment because she was a bad person. This is what we call *'self-blame'* and is a common issue for people dealing with childhood sexual abuse, domestic violence or other traumatic events. The guilt, that belonged to those who had hurt her, became hers. The shame she felt became the trigger point for her rebellion. She would never have considered forgiving her parents, because in her eyes, she was the wrongdoer.

Alina is one of many individuals who have encountered mistreatment, rejection, or betrayal by those they trusted and relied upon for protection. As we listen to their stories, our natural reaction is to be outraged by the injustice of their experience, and to identify with and affirm their right to remain angry, bitter, confused and fearful.

Did you notice, however, that Alina had subconsciously and subtly shifted from being solely a *victim* to also becoming a *persecutor*? Through her behaviour, she punished her father, her mother, her teachers, her peers, her husband, and her children ... and, of course, herself. Why? Because no matter how valid our emotional reactions may seem, when negative feelings and thoughts are internalised, they often lead us to act in hurtful ways toward others.

# #2. WOUNDEDNESS ... CAUSED BY OUR INTERNALISED NEGATIVE EMOTIONS AND OUR BEHAVIOURAL REACTION TO THE EVENT.

Albert's story:

"I was the youngest of three sons born into a working-class family, in Melbourne during the 1940's. For as long as I can remember, I was an anxious child. What I didn't understand then, was that even as a baby, I had become the target of both of my brothers' brutality. As I grew, they found many new ways of abusing me emotionally, physically and sexually. As a little child I looked to my mum for protection but because she worked full time, she was often not there. Her absence contributed to the fear I had of my brothers.

"By the time I'd reached my teens, my brothers had joined a street gang. They recruited me and forced me to become a courier, delivering messages, money and drugs to other gang leaders and underworld figures. I did what they asked, because I was more afraid of them, than I was of the police. Eventually, all three of us found employment in the same industry, and my brothers became enforcers in the Union to which we, and our fellow employees belonged to.

"By this time, I had become a lot taller and stronger than my siblings, which resulted in them ceasing their harassment of me. Regrettably, I developed a dependence on alcohol to manage my anxiety. Subsequently, when I was charged with driving under the influence, the magistrate identified me as an alcoholic and ordered my rehabilitation at the Salvation Army.

*"One morning at work, I was informed that one of my brothers had been murdered the night before, and the other had gone into hiding for his safety. I believed that because I was related to the murdered man, I would also be a target. All I could think of doing was to run. I had heard from a girl I knew, about a Retreat Centre about 100 kms from Melbourne, and I ended up there.*

*"When I arrived, I chose not to tell them at first that I was afraid for my life, unless of course ... they refused to help me. In no time I discovered that it was a Christian Retreat Centre, and that one of the staff was a counsellor. I soon began having regular sessions with him. He helped me understand that some of my bad decisions and dysfunctional behaviours were a direct consequence of the painful emotions and destructive thought patterns that I had developed during my life in a brutal family.*

*"The counselling was extremely helpful, but despite this, I continued making bad decisions — frequently leaving the Centre in my first year and resuming binge drinking. However, I kept returning to the Centre. It was the only safe place I had ever known. The love and kindness of the people at the centre, and the counselling, led me to consider what made them so caring and compassionate. I eventually committed my life to Christ and embraced their Christian belief and lifestyle. I overcame my alcohol addiction.*

*"As a result of my transformation, I was extended an invitation to join the staff. I accepted and had five great years there before meeting the lady who became my wife, and this wonderful event led me back to a life in suburban Melbourne."*

People in similar situations such as Albert, are imprisoned by lies. Lies told by the *hurters* and confirmed by many life experiences:

*"You are bad!"*
*"You are worthless!"*
*"Now see what you have done!"*

When they eventually learn the truth, it appears unbelievable. They seem powerless at first to accept the new truthful reality — *that the first step towards healing a wounded spirit* — is recognising that the responsibility for the event lies with the perpetrator.

The second truth — *is that the responsibility for the reactions to the event and the behaviours that emanate from that reaction* — lies with the wounded person.

When we are prepared to accept these truths, we are empowered to move the guilt we have falsely carried ... to where it belongs ... and to embrace the responsibility for our own responses. This is what Albert did, and he described it as "*the prison doors swinging open and he walks free for the first time in his life.*"

## #3. WOUNDEDNESS BECAUSE OF OUR OWN BEHAVIOURS, WHICH RESULT FROM INTERNALISING OUR NEGATIVE REACTIONS TO THE EVENT.

Referring back to Bella's Story:

Emotional pain in families and communities often stem

from the victim's reactions to past events rather than the events themselves. We remember speaking to a lady we will call Bella. She told us that she never walked around her neighbourhood or nearby botanical garden or at the beach. When we asked her why she never walked in these places, she said that she was afraid of dogs.

We inquired if she had ever been bitten by a dog, to which she replied, no. She added that her father kept large dogs to guard his factory premises and that she loved them and played with them every day after school. We were puzzled, so we then asked her what she was afraid of as a child.

She surprised us by saying, "It is not *what* I was afraid of, but *who*? I was very afraid of my father. He was an angry man back then and his voice and general manner intimidated me."

When we asked her whether she was still afraid of her father, she chuckled and told us that on the contrary she loved him and trusted him implicitly.

In that moment — both we and she — immediately understood what had happened. She had not actually overcome her fear of her father; she had subconsciously transferred her fear onto what she most strongly identified with her father — dogs.

To overcome her current phobia, she needed to address her historic fear of her father. She needed to speak about her fear, to her father or a counsellor. She needed to forgive her father for being so angry and intimidating, and to reaffirm the love and trust she now felt toward him.

Some months later we heard that she had done that, and her fear of dogs was gradually dissipating.

Bella's story helps us understand that many of our intentional and unintentional behaviours are the result of internalising our reaction to a painful event in our lives. These negative emotions keep us on high alert, which means a heightened state of anxiety. It might express itself as phobic behaviours ... including specific fears like agoraphobia or eating disorders such as anorexia nervosa or bulimia nervosa. It may heighten aggressive behaviours or result in acute social isolation. A person who is living in a heightened state of anxiety will often require both medical and psychological intervention.

# FOR FURTHER REFLECTION

Before proceeding, please reflect on the two questions that Graeme was asked to address.

#1 "Do you believe that God, your Creator and Father freely offers forgiveness to you for every sin you have ever committed on the basis that Jesus Christ willingly suffered and died for each of them?"

#2 "Do you believe that God, your Creator and Father freely offers forgiveness to every person who has ever hurt you ... on the basis that Jesus Christ willingly suffered and died for every sin they have ever committed against you?"

Chapter Three

# Only Way Forward

## *The second answer to the question: 'why forgive?'*
## *... is because to forgive may be the only way to deal with resentment.*

Another answer to the question '**WHY FORGIVE?**', lies in the possibility that there is no other way to deal with deeply internalised resentment. The woundedness it inflicts and fosters, leaves no other way than to forgive the person who hurt us.

In the first chapter we described ourselves — and millions of others — as 'experts' on resentment. This is certainly not true of any of us when it comes to forgiveness. Although more than forty years have passed since we experienced the joy of Graeme being set free from his own prison of resentment, through forgiving the person he had always held responsible for his pain; together we are still discovering the depth and beauty and transforming power of this life-giving gift of God.

Being set free from the prison of resentment does not make us experts … but simply disciples of the One, who in the darkest hour of His life, forgave those who falsely accused Him, tortured Him and ultimately killed Him. We are learning more every day by simply obeying our Master's commands, "*Love … as you have been loved.*" "*Forgive … as you have been forgiven.*" And "*Accept others, as God-in-Christ has accepted you.*"

Graeme has shared how the first sixteen years of our marriage were often painful for Julia who was frequently puzzled and hurt by his outbursts of anger. Julia takes up that part of our story.

> *"That is true, but the relevant issue is how I dealt with my painful emotions. The truth is that I internalised them, just as Graeme had done, but instead of expressing them in anger, I went silent — sometimes for long periods of time. He experienced my silence as punishment. Without realising it at the time, my response to being hurt, was to internalise my feelings, and then respond to my husband by engaging in the destructive behaviour of emotional withdrawal. My response, it turns out, was in fact identical to Graeme's. I needed God's forgiveness — as well as Graeme's — as much as he needed mine.*
>
> *"I gradually began to understand that when our heavenly Father was rejected and sinned against by the humans He created, He was understandably angry. However, God's anger is the opposite to ours. Whilst our anger frequently leads us into unkind, unhelpful behaviour, like aggression or going silent, God's anger leads to mercy. He always chooses to respond with mercy and compassion. He expresses that mercy through unconditional love and forgiveness, and he commands and empowers us to love and forgive others as He has loved and forgiven us.*

*"I began to understand something else. When I was willing to obey the command to love and forgive Graeme, just as God in Christ had loved and forgiven me, it not only changed my behaviour, but it helped create an environment that made it easier for both of us to apologise and forgive, whilst reaffirming that we loved each other and were both determined to grow into better humans."*

Listen to the Apostle Paul in Ephesians 4:29-32. *'Don't use foul or abusive language. Let everything you say be good and helpful, so that your words will be an encouragement to those who hear them. And do not bring sorrow to God's Holy Spirit by the way you live. Remember, He has identified you as His own, guaranteeing that you will be saved on the day of redemption. Get rid of all bitterness, rage, anger, harsh words and slander as well as all types of evil behaviour. Instead, be kind to each other, tender-hearted, forgiving one another, just as God through Christ has forgiven you.'*

*"When I experienced the freedom that forgiving Graeme and others gave me, I knew, that while hurt and offence is inevitable — God has provided the only truly healthy way to escape the consequences of remaining angry and resentful."*

This passage from Ephesians serves both as the 'Christian's Statement of Goals' and as our 'Charter of Values.' Included among the list of goals for today's Christian man and woman, are to use helpful, encouraging language, to build each other up and to rid ourselves of all rage, bitterness, resentment and malice. The key values are kindness, compassion, and forgiveness. In the very next verse Paul tells us how we achieve these goals and attain to these values. *'Be imitators of God therefore, as dearly loved children and live a life of love, just as Christ loved us and gave Himself up for us as a fragrant offering and sacrifice.'*

Psychologists for some time now, have increasingly recognised forgiveness as a valuable therapeutic tool for emotional healing. This has led to the development of several definitions of forgiveness. A summary of a broadly accepted psychological understanding of forgiveness is as follows:

- *Forgiveness* is a conscious decision to let go of anger and resentment towards someone who has wronged you, without excusing or forgetting what happened.

- *Forgiveness* is a personal choice. It is not about forgetting. It can help you move on.

- *Forgiveness* can lead to understanding, empathy and even compassion. It is not minimizing your hurt. It is not the same as pardoning.

- *Forgiveness* can help you repair a damaged relationship, but it does not obligate you to reconcile with the person who harmed you.

- Pursuing justice through punishment or compensation, can coexist with *forgiveness.*

Theologians, Christian psychologists, and counsellors concur with every aspect of this definition. Our interpretations of forgiveness, however, incorporate an additional dimension ... grounded in the profound truth that our relationship with God is made possible through Christ's sacrifice for the sins of humanity. God forgives us through Jesus Christ's death and resurrection, adopting us as His children. He then commands and empowers us to forgive others in the same way as He forgives us.

The definition we have formulated goes like this:

*"We forgive another ...*
*when we lay down our resentment and our desire for revenge ...*
*and set the other person free from the obligation to suffer for the wrongs they have committed against us ...*
*just as God has set us free from the obligation to suffer for the wrongs we have committed against Him."*

What we like about this definition is that it highlights that the act of forgiving is not dependent on human logic, strength of character or positive thinking. It is based on gratitude and obedience. Therefore, as beneficiaries of this unprompted and unwarranted forgiveness, our appropriate response is to express perpetual gratitude. When our divine Forgiver asks us to forgive others, He empowers us to do something that would be otherwise impossible.

The reality is that many people reject both the Psychologists' and Counsellors' assertion that forgiveness is the only antidote to the deadly poison of resentment and look for other remedies. They seek out alternate remedies such as:

- **Escapism.** Individuals who experience significant distress may isolate themselves and engage in activities such as substance abuse, viewing pornographic material, or creating imaginary scenarios.

- **Anger and revenge seeking.** These behaviours always cause hurt to the people who love us and seek to support us.

- **Self-condemning behaviour.** Putting ourselves down.

- **Self-criticism.** Carrying blame and shame that is not ours to carry.

- **Comfort and Affirmation seeking.** Engaging in numerous relationships, built on seeking comfort rather than giving love.

- **Projection of painful emotions ...** transferring past events into the present and the future. Allowing our anxieties and our resentment to negatively impact our family relationships, our employment and our lives in the broader community.

In an address given at the Vatican, Danny and Leila Abdallah spoke of forgiveness as "the path to holiness." As we reflect on this phrase, it begins to broaden our understanding of forgiveness even more. Our Heavenly Father commands us many times to relate to others in a fashion that reflect the very ways He relates to us. Here are just a few of our thoughts:

- Love one another (John 13:34)
- Honour one another (Romans 12:10)

- Accept one another (Romans 15:7)
- Forgive one another (Ephesians 4:32)
- Comfort one another (1 Thessalonians 4:18)
- Encourage one another (1 Thessalonians 5:11)
- Care for one another (1 Corinthians 12:25)
- Bear with one another (Colossians 3:13)

**Loving. Honouring. Accepting. Forgiving. Comforting. Encouraging. Caring. Being Patient.**

He relates to us daily in all these ways, and by doing the same toward others, we become more like Him. It becomes obvious that none of these things are optional extras. They are essential qualities of followers of Christ.

# FOR FURTHER REFLECTION

We invite you to reflect on the difference between the way we respond to feeling angry and the way God responds. Our behaviour when we are angry is usually toward being destructive. God's response is toward being merciful.

- Do you agree that to forgive or not to forgive is a personal choice?

- Ephesians chapter 4 helps us understand that we need to adopt a 'Statement of Goals' and a 'Charter of Values'. The goals God requires us to set for ourselves are:

a) to build others up rather than tear them down
b) to let everything we say be good and helpful
c) to encourage others
d) to get rid of all bitterness, rage, anger, harsh words and slander and all types of evil behaviour
e) the values we are to adopt are kindness, tender heartedness and forgiveness

If you have chosen *not* to forgive, what alternative strategies have you adopted?
Are they working for you?
Are they working for the people you love?

Chapter Four

# Wounds and Scars

## *The third answer to the question: 'why forgive?'*
## *... is that forgiveness helps us differentiate between wounds and scars.*

When we live with unresolved resentment toward people in the past, we carry our wounds into every phase of our lives and every relationship in our present and in our future. Conversely, each instance of forgiving those who have wronged us, enhances our ability to live the remainder of our lives in the liberty of forgiveness, and extends this capacity to assist others in achieving the same.

We commence this chapter with a surprising truth.

## *Wounds can be healed ...*
## *but scars may remain.*

In chapter 20 of John's Gospel, we read of Jesus' first meeting with his disciples on the evening of the day of His resurrection. They had locked themselves in a room because they were afraid that they too might be arrested and crucified. Suddenly, Jesus appears in the room without unlocking the door — and of course — the disciples are all terrified.

He reassures them and encourages them to examine the marks on his hands, which were caused by the nails, and to observe his side where the soldier's spear had pierced him. The scars were both the evidence of his humanity and his suffering. The Apostle John tells us that Thomas, one of the twelve disciples, was not present in the room that day, and when those who *were* there told him that they had seen the Lord, he was naturally, sceptical.

Like others who spent time in the city of Jerusalem, he was familiar with the brutality of crucifixions. No-one comes back from such a grisly death! Moreover, were there not people who had witnessed Jesus being interred in a tomb which was then sealed with an immovable stone at its entrance? Thomas said to his friends, "Unless I see and touch the prints of the nails in his hands and put my hand in the wound in his side, I will not believe."

Seven days later, the disciples were back in the same locked room, and suddenly Jesus appeared again. This time, Thomas was with them. Jesus said to Thomas. "Put your finger here ... see my hands. Reach out your hand and put it into the wound in my side. Stop doubting and believe." Jesus was saying, "Hey Thomas! It's me! I was dead! I am now alive! I have the scars to prove it!" Thomas said to him. "My Lord and my God".

The nails and the spear — both tools of the crucifixion and symbols of humanity's cruel rejection of him — were gone. The pain and suffering were in the past. Sin and death were overcome through His sacrificial death. The stone was removed from the grave, and Christ the redeemer was resurrected. The wounding of Jesus had finished ... but His scars remained.

For many of us, the circumstance that was the cause of wounding in our lives is no longer present. If that is the case for you, we want you to know the wounding is over. The verbal, physical and sexual abuse has ceased. Rejection and fear, once an inevitable part of everyday life — has finished.

Forgiveness can completely remove the power and control that a person or circumstance had over your life. The scars remind you of what the love and grace of God has enabled you to do and will continue to do. They are both a reminder of what you have been through, and the strength God gave you to break free and to begin a new chapter in your life.

You may have escaped from a marriage in which you have/had endured years of physical or emotional abuse and manipulation. You may have lived with fearful anticipation of the next violent event.

## *It is finished!*

You, and your children are safe at last. You have dealt with your hurt and anger by forgiving your partner, who may still refuse to accept responsibility for his or her behaviour. There will be no going back to this toxic relationship. The wounding has ceased. The scars may remain as a reminder of God's loving intervention and of your resolve and courage.

What are these scars? Well, you might still have emotional defence mechanisms that were once useful for protection ... but now are unnecessary. You may feel excited by your new freedom but apprehensive about being a single parent. You are now safe from the physical and verbal abuse of the past but nervous about being the sole provider and decision maker for your family. You may have anxiety about building new friendships or relationships although you are determined to do so. You may lack confidence in your ability to succeed at life, but each time you achieve a new goal your confidence grows. The wounding has ceased. The scars remain, but each day they can become less debilitating and more empowering.

If we mistake the scars of past wounds, as new or remaining wounds that need healing, rather than testimonies of survival and reasons for pursuing even greater transformation, then we will continue to search for something we already have.

There will be times when disappointing events occur or when we feel rejected, criticised or betrayed. If our wounds have become scars, we may need to explore various strategies that will enable us to navigate our way through these experiences, so that they will neither trigger negative responses related to old wounds, or trap us in a new prison of resentment.

One of the most common scars is shame. If this is the case we may not only need to experience the importance of forgiving another, but also the joy and freedom the process of forgiving ourselves brings.

In a recent conservation, someone made the following statement: *"that the concept of forgiving ourselves is irrelevant to the follower of Jesus."* His reason for saying that was, *"If God has forgiven us ... that is all that matters, not whether we forgive ourselves."*

I politely disagreed with him on the basis that if God has forgiven me ... and I still have not forgiven myself ... then I am withholding something from myself that God has freely given me. It means that I have a controversy with God. I cannot and must not refuse to forgive myself, any more than

I can refuse to forgive the person who wounded me.

Why? Because the responsibility of those who stand in the presence of a loving God who forgives us unconditionally — is to be as generous in loving and forgiving of both ourselves and others — just as our Heavenly Father is.

## FOR FURTHER REFLECTION

The concept of wounds and scars can be confusing. Properly understood however, it can be very helpful reflecting on where we have been and where we are now. Some of the healthy thought patterns and life skills that are part of who we are now, have their origins in the whole journey we have been on, not just the place we are currently in our journey.

Consider the important lessons in your life you have learnt from. What might be a leftover scar as result of a deeply wounding experience?

Pause now ... and give thanks for them.

## Chapter Five

# When it is Time

# WHEN IS IT TIME TO FORGIVE?

Consider Colin's story:

*"I was sexually abused in my early teens, but back then I did not realise how serious it was. The abuse, by an older man in a position of trust occurred when he drove me home from music practice. I did not initiate the sexual contact, and it was pleasurable — shrewdly cloaked in a camouflage of harmlessness. So, in my head, it was happening with my agreement and seemed harmless to me.*

*"I did not discuss what was happening with anyone, and I had no inkling of the subtle shame that was attached to it. The abusive acts continued for a few years, becoming more uncomfortable and even more unacceptable to me as I matured. Eventually I dropped music practice and thus avoided the abusive routine. The memories of these events however, felt increasingly awkward and shameful.*

*"As a young man I acquired a position in a bank prior to commencing two years of National Service. After this I returned to the bank, married, had two beautiful daughters and took a few positions of responsibility within the local church. Life seemed quite rosy.*

*"Meanwhile, I had no idea of the subconscious impact that the abuse was wreaking in my social life.*

*Over the next few decades, the feelings of shame were further submerged by the responsibilities and commitments associated with family, work, and church activities. This busyness was further intensified, by the launching of my own business, which began in our home before I transitioned it to a rented facility and engaged three employees.*

*"I loyally and earnestly participated in the ministry of my Church, still unaware of the subconscious wounds in play. I attended multiple weekly services, participated in a brass band and choir practices and assumed the demanding role of Church treasurer. During all this busyness, I experienced the stress and heartache of a marriage split which eventually led to a divorce.*

*"Sometime after the divorce, I began to pray that God would bring a godly woman into my life, who as my wife, would join me in drawing closer to Him. He answered my prayers and blessed me with the sweetest and loveliest follower of Jesus, to whom I have been married for 38 years.*

*"When we married, I entered this new phase of my life with the 'victim shame' still deeply internalised, until a life changing event occurred about two decades ago. During my participation in the 'Growing to Maturity' discipleship course, I was prompted to reflect on various life events. This review helped me identify past traumas that were adversely impacting me without my awareness. God prompted me to revisit the memory of the sexual*

events that occurred during my teens. As I did that, I received a revelation from God, that those events had left deeply imprinted and painful wounds on my heart and mind.

"I shared the revelations with my wife and as we prayed together. I understood for the first time, that what had seemed harmless at the time, had indeed, been sexual abuse. A man in a position of authority had patiently groomed me and taken advantage of my compliant nature and my immaturity. As I reflected on my life, I realised how the abuse had affected me.

"For almost six decades, I had shied away from maintaining lasting male friendships. Casting my mind back over the years, I had cordial relationships with many males, none of which had led to long term friendships. The reality was that my friendships with my peers in primary school, secondary college, workplaces, the military, in churches and in my neighbourhood had all faded from view. I also became aware that I had always felt a tangible discomfort whenever I mingled with men in a social setting, whether at parties, at church or at other events. It was a discomfort which I did not feel whilst in the company of women.

"The woundedness I am describing, I realise had also impacted my relationship with Jesus, Himself. I can remember grappling with scriptures that encouraged me to relate to Jesus as a friend. Reflecting on my experiences during my teenage *years, made me feel uneasy.*

*"As a Christian, I knew that I had a choice. I could forgive my abuser as Christ had forgiven me — or I could turn my anxieties into a prison of resentment and anger. I chose the former.*

*"In a wonderful way the process of forgiveness had already begun. I had moved the responsibility for the event from myself to my abuser. The guilt and shame were his — not mine. I now knew that he was responsible for his actions, but now I was responsible for my response to that truth. Having received unconditional forgiveness from God, I extended forgiveness to my abuser in the same manner that Christ forgave me.*

*"Although in my heart I knew I had forgiven him, I felt a strong desire to be able to express my forgiveness to him face to face. The problem was I did not know whether he was still alive, or even if he was ... where he lived. God had it all in hand!*

*"Not long after I had forgiven him, my mother passed away. The funeral was held at the Church where I had grown up as a boy — and to my amazement — the man who had abused me, was among the mourners. During the service, my heart was pounding, as I sweated on how to approach him and what I would say.*

*"Later, during the refreshments I noticed him leaving the church. I followed him and managed to*

*confront him with what he had done to me. He seemed surprised that I was raising it with him and played down its significance, saying to me that nobody had got hurt. I held my ground, asserted how I had been wounded, and emphasised that I had forgiven him, just as God had forgiven me.*

*"He hurried away, still playing down the significance of the events, while I went back into the church, knowing that I was free and feeling that a great weight had been lifted from my shoulders. I cannot say what effect my words of forgiveness had on the man I forgave, but I can testify that my obedience had made a huge difference to me. My heart was incredibly lighter.*

*"Since forgiving the man who had abused me as a boy, I can reflect on what has changed. I am thanking God that my woundedness has subsided significantly and I am confident that it will continue to do so. I am pleased that I can now mingle with men socially without discomfort. I have enjoyed attending men's breakfasts and fellowship gatherings. I have now started intentional and meaningful friendships with other men.*

*"I have been able to reinforce my relationship with Jesus, as my heavenly friend, my brother, my Saviour and my Lord of Lords — totally disconnected from the awkward sexual memories of my teens. Although it is not always possible or advisable for all survivors to confront their perpetrator, in my case it was beneficial. I am grateful that circumstances*

*allowed me to convey both my pain and forgiveness to the individual who had harmed me".*

Colin's story is a powerful example of one who, although he was vaguely aware of his woundedness, had unconsciously internalised his shame and confusion for a large part of his life.

However, when challenged by the leaders of the course that he undertook, and assisted by his wife; he had the courage to revisit the events of the past and came to understand the connection between his abuse as a teenager and his adult anxieties. When he did so, he took immediate action to resolve the issue by forgiving the man who had abused him so long ago.

This was the moment in his life when he discovered the '*Why* and '*When*' of forgiveness. For him there was no other way to be set free from his anxieties. That was his answer to the question, "Why Forgive?"

The answer to the question '*When should I forgive?*" came the moment he understood the connection between his abuse as a teen, and the anxieties he had experienced his entire adult life. If he was to escape the damaging impact of his internalised shame, then he needed to move that shame from himself to the abuser and then forgive him. And he needed to forgive him *now*, even though the abuse had occurred decades ago.

In deciding 'when should I forgive?' ... a helpful question to ask ourselves is, "*Who is currently paying the price for my choice not to forgive?*" You can be sure that the answer will always be '*myself* and '*those who I love the most.*' Along with us, they will be the joint beneficiaries of us forgiving the person who caused our hurt.

Forgiveness typically does not happen instantly. It is not common for individuals to immediately understand the necessity of addressing the harm, at the time of injury. Additionally, it is not always apparent immediately, that such actions are necessary.

There comes a time when individuals recognize they can either continue feeling angry and resentful — or choose to forgive. The answer to the question *'when should I forgive?'* is clearly — *as soon as I recognise the negative impact on my life and my relationships of NOT doing so.*

Before we move on to How to Forgive, let us summarise the reasons we have mentioned so far, as to why people, when faced with the choice to forgive or not to forgive, choose the latter.

1. They do not understand what forgiveness is.

2. They feel that it is unjust and unfair that the perpetrator receives forgiveness while they continue to live with the consequences of what the perpetrator has done to them or their loved ones.

3. They believe that in some way they are justly punishing the person who wronged them, by maintaining their rage.

4. They do not understand the connection between past hurts and the emotional or psychological damage they are currently experiencing.

5. They do not understand that their bitterness and resentment is not a consequence of being hurt by another ... but rather the result of the choice they have made not to forgive.

6. They believe that the primary beneficiary of forgiveness is the person who receives it. This seems unfair and undeserved.

7. They do not understand that their anger and bitterness is negatively impacting their valued relationships.

8. The hurtful event may have happened so long ago they cannot see the relevance of forgiveness.

9. They do not understand or obey the biblical command found in Colossians 3:12-13. *"Since God chose you to be the holy people He loves, you must clothe yourselves with tender-hearted mercy, kindness, humility, gentleness, and patience. Make allowance for each other's faults and forgive anyone who offends you. Remember, the Lord forgave you, so you must forgive others."*

# FOR FURTHER REFLECTION

The answer to the question, "when should I forgive", *is the moment I realise that my resentment is negatively impacting my life and my relationships.* Forgiveness is a process which should begin when you become aware of the negative impact resentment is having on your life. Remember, forgiveness is for *your* sake."

Pause and reflect on the reasons why people find it difficult to forgive or not to forgive. Does one or more of them apply to you?

## Chapter Six

# Prepare Yourself

# PREPARING YOURSELF TO FORGIVE ANOTHER

## #1. EXAMINE THE CONSEQUENCES OF STAYING ANGRY

Case # 1. John believed that his father had rejected him when he deserted his family to live with another woman. He internalised his hurt and spoke to no-one about it. Now, as an adult, the internalised pain had emerged as insecurity, anxiety, and anger. His wife had left him, fearful that he would hurt her and the children. Several relationships followed his divorce, but they all ended for the same reason.

Case # 2. Mary had been bullied as a teenager at secondary school. She became so fearful that she became a school refuser. She left school early and worked in a bakery. She soon left that job and others because of anxiety. As an adult she discovered that the only thing that relieved her anxiety was alcohol. She eventually became alcohol dependent and is now unemployed and homeless.

Case # 3. Max, who as a boy, had been continuously criticised and ridiculed by his father, was recently sacked from his employment as a sales representative. The reason for his dismissal was his 'uncontrolled aggression' and his 'inability to collaborate harmoniously with a team.' He had been the subject of complaints from female colleagues, of bullying, harassment and verbal abuse.

Each of these three people could describe themselves as victims of other people's unkindness. *The stark truth, however, is that their behaviours are not primarily the result of being abandoned or abused by others. Their painful emotions and damaging behaviours are the direct result of them remaining angry, and in most cases internalising their anger, guilt and shame.*

Internalised anger negatively affects our mental and physical health. It impedes our ability to make good decisions. It has the capacity to ruin relationships, render us unemployable, lead us into unhelpful dependencies, and increase the probability that we will become violent.

Angry people may withdraw from social interaction, adopt a cynical view of the world and engage in constant criticism of others. They may become difficult spouses, unpredictable parents and disagreeable neighbours. They are prone to depression, unacceptable bouts of rage and a crippling anxiety that may cause them to respond to others in defensive and self-protective ways.

Internalised anger, as a response to being wounded by others, leads to nowhere good. But there is hope …

*That hope comes from a shift in our mindset. It is the willingness to understand, that when we have been used, abused, manipulated or exploited by another person or a set of circumstances beyond our control … anger is only one of many responses we can make … and certainly … the costliest!*

## #2. UNDERSTAND HOW SELF-BLAME & FEAR AFFECT YOU.

Closely aligned to internalised anger is what we have called *'self-blame.'* This commonly occurs for survivors of childhood sexual abuse, sole survivors of an accident or other traumatic events, or parents of children who have died. It is characterised by the *'if only'* questions, or the *'I can never forgive myself'* statements.

In sexual abuse and domestic violence situations, convincing the victim that it is their fault, is part of the perpetrators strategy to silence the victim. In *'sole-survivor'* situations, guilt is the belief: that in some way my survival cost the lives of others. For those who ask the *'if only'* question it is the belief that they had it in their power to prevent the traumatic event, and they failed to do so. Whatever the reason for accepting the guilt and shame — it is a destructive and erroneous decision.

"When I (Graeme) share my story, I often explain that in my early twenties as a young pastor, I would from time to time attend Pastors' conferences. As soon as I was in the presence of other pastors, I would feel inferior to all of them. In my mind I could convince myself that I was their equal, but the shame I had felt since I was a child, convinced me that I was inferior to them and sooner or later, they would discover that I was a fake, with a shameful secret."

The truth is that *'self-blame'* is much more difficult to address than the *'real guilt'* we might feel when we have actually wronged someone. In the latter, we have the option of apologising for our actions and in most cases being forgiven by them. We also have the option of confessing our sinful behaviour to God and receiving His unlimited and unconditional forgiveness. However, when we have chosen to carry shame that is not our own, we feel like there is no way to deal with it. We cannot really apologise for something we have done wrong, because we, in our minds are both the victim and the perpetrator.

#3. FOCUS ON FORGIVING THOSE WHO HURT YOU.

There are several reasons that we might stubbornly and actively resist the idea of forgiving a person who has hurt us. It is helpful to be able to recognise the reasons and seek to understand what God is really calling us to do.

*To many people ... painful memories have become an indispensable part of their lives.*
*They cannot imagine life without them.*

The truth is that when we do forgive, we do not forget. We cannot by choice, erase memories. They will always be somewhere in our conscious or sub-conscious mind and will be subject to certain triggers. We know instinctively, that forgiving someone for a behaviour that has left us hurt or traumatised, will not erase the memory of the hurtful event. It will only take the reminder of a certain place or a particular name, or sight or smell and the memories associated with the painful experience will flood back, and with them all the rejection, or injustice, or fear, or woundedness that you felt at the time.

What most people do not realise, is that whilst forgiving a perpetrator does not erase the memory of what they have done to us, forgiveness has the power to convert the negative effects of a painful memory into a life transforming force. We want to illustrate what we mean by sharing another part of Graeme's story.

*"When Julia and I were returning to Australia from the United States, after I had experienced the joy of forgiveness, I was hit by a very disturbing thought. For many years when I went out on the road, I would frequently see a transport truck, with the name of the company displayed on it. It happened that that name was the same as the name of the person I had always blamed for the anger I carried. The thought that occurred to me enroute somewhere between USA and Australia, was that those trucks would still be there, and that name would raise the same feelings it had always raised, and that it would mean that I had not really forgiven that person, and that I was not truly free.*

*"I was very anxious about that and sure enough we had not been back in Australia very long before it happened. I need to tell you, the truck and the name it carried, did evoke the same feelings it had always done, and I was aware of the all too familiar anger. At the same time, however, I found myself thanking God that these painful feelings reminded me that I had forgiven that person and that I was on a new journey to health and wholeness. Every time, thereafter, when it occurred, I would thank God for the power of forgiveness and in time the memories lost their negative power and became a memorial to my healing."*

What we have discovered is ... that painful memories are like tombstones that remind us of pain and loss.

When we forgive the perpetrator, God transforms our tombstones into milestones — reminders of how far we've come since we passed the last one.

# FOR FURTHER REFLECTION

Preparing yourself to forgive another involves:

(a) examining the consequences of holding on to anger

(b) becoming aware of how internalised negative emotions can and will affect you and your relationships

(c) releasing the mistaken belief that you must forget the hurtful event in order to forgive

By doing these things, you can turn your tombstones into milestones.

Each one of these steps is important. If you decide to take them, would you attempt it on your own or ask somebody to help you? If the latter, who would you ask?

## Chapter Seven

# Broken Saw

# ANOTHER INSPIRING TRUE STORY

In the mid 1980's, Greg and Ria had chosen to step out in faith and engage in children's ministry, thereby opening themselves up to experience God's provision in various ways. They had three young children, a mortgage, and a car ... but no guaranteed income apart from casual jobs.

Greg and Ria (not their real names) had asked Barry — a builder-friend from their church about some ideas for renovations on their house.

Barry came and visited them, offering some insightful suggestions about relocating the kitchen to the front veranda and creating a third bedroom where the kitchen was located.

Greg says, *"We were excited about what he had proposed and trusted his work, as he had previously done some renovations on behalf of our church for us, to convert our garage into a workshop/office for our kids ministry."*

Barry promised that he would keep their costs as low as possible by using recycled materials and offering a minimal labour charge. It was agreed by a handshake of trust between fellow Christians.

Ria picks up the story. *"In no time Barry came, and our day-to-day living was soon disrupted. For at least two weeks we had no kitchen whilst trying to maintain the regular* routine for our primary-school-aged children and our ministry commitments. At the time, Greg was teaching Christian Religious Education (CRE) in a local school and, we also led a team of volunteers running an after-school Bible club in the same school, and served as Kids' Pastors in our church."

Greg continues. *"A few weeks into the renovations I was on my way to teach my CRE class. Hurriedly, I jumped into my van parked in the driveway and put it into reverse. I had only backed a very short distance, when there was a loud crunching noise."*

Greg had run over Barry's circular saw, which had been left on the ground behind the back wheel of the van. Barry raced outside to examine the damage.

Neither man was very happy ... Greg was now running late for his class ... and Barry had lost his circular saw. Both men regarded the other as responsible for what happened. Greg reasoned that the saw should never have been left where it was ... and Barry blamed Greg for not looking behind the vehicle before moving. In the haste and heat of the moment, Barry demanded that Greg and Ria replace the saw at the cost of $200.

Greg says, *"We were flabbergasted by both the blame and the demand. It seemed unfair. We spoke with our Pastor in the hope that he might act as a mediator and negotiate a compromise. To our surprise, he simply advised that we show grace to Barry and pay him the money."*

Ria continues. *"We had to skimp on some of our weekly groceries to write a cheque for $200. The next day Greg handed over the cheque, with an apology for any inconvenience caused. Barry accepted the compensation and very quickly finished up the area of work he was doing at the time. He then packed up his tools and left, never to return — which meant that the rest of the renovations were left unfinished!*

*"We looked at our situation ... incomplete renovations ... a fractured relationship ... now $200 short for daily necessities ... and an uncertainty as to how we would be able to finish off the internal renovations to an acceptable standard. We had been obedient in showing grace, but we were puzzled as to what else we should do.*

*"So, we began to pray for the Lord's blessing on Barry and his family and his business. Although initially, it was difficult, we continued to pray and release Barry from any bitterness and blame. We soon realised however, that in doing so, we were also being released from being imprisoned by the negative emotions that we had initially experienced."*

Greg adds, *"We continued to pray for God's blessing on Barry, and over the next couple of years with the help of neighbours and friends, and the Lord's provision of money and materials, we were able to complete our renovations to our satisfaction.*

*"Strange as it may seem, almost two years after the incident — Barry pulled into our driveway. We welcomed him in, and over a coffee we caught up on each other's family*

news. To our surprise, Barry then pulled out his cheque book and wrote a cheque for $200. He apologised for being so unreasonable about the broken saw. Although he did not apologise for leaving the renovations unfinished, we gratefully accepted his gesture of compensation.

"Over the years, we have had many opportunities to share this story with people as a demonstration of the power of forgiveness and grace."

Greg and Ria's story illustrates the truth that offences and hurts can happen in any one of the many areas of our lives. Their prompt forgiveness of Barry was made possible because of their strong commitment to the fact that God had completely forgiven them and commanded them to forgive others in the same way. They chose not to allow the monetary cost or the inconvenience of the unfinished renovations to be a source of resentment. Just as important is the fact that it led to Barry reaching out to them ... albeit two years later.

## Chapter Eight

# FAQ's

# FREQUENTLY ASKED QUESTIONS

- *What is resentment?*

Resentment is best described as a complex, multilayered emotional reaction to being mistreated or wronged by another person, situation or series of circumstances. Often resentment feels like a merging of anger, bitterness, disgust, disappointment and disapproval toward the person or events that led your perspective. (Psychologist Susan Albers. PsyD.)

- *What are some of life's circumstances that can trigger resentment?*

Being taken advantage of by others. Being put down, dismissed or ignored by significant others. Feeling inadequate, overlooked or unheard. Having unrealistic expectations of others or the world around you. Maintaining relationships with those who always put their needs before your own. Interactions with those who undermine your authority.

- *What are the common indications that resentment is impacting our lives?*

Your negative emotions keep resurfacing. Anger becomes a perennial issue in relating to others. You feel there is no closure for your painful response to a hurtful event. You have feelings of regret and remorse. Increasing feelings of anxiety and the tendency towards emotional withdrawal.

- *How do I let go of resentment?*

The answer is FORGIVENESS. We suggest that you reread chapter six and seriously consider following the steps that will enable you to forgive the person (or persons) you are resentful toward.

- *Does my forgiveness of the perpetrator pardon them for the wrong committed against me?*

*NO!*

Forgiveness does not release the wrongdoer from their accountability, nor does it remove any obligations they might have in relation to the law. At best when a person receives undeserved forgiveness it might bring them to repentance for their wrongful behaviour, so opening the way for reconciliation.

- *What does the word repentance mean?*

Webster's Dictionary defines repentance this way:

1. To feel sorry or self-reproachful for what one has done or failed to do; be conscience stricken or contrite.

2. To feel such regret or dissatisfaction over some action or intention as to change one's mind or behaviours.

3. To feel so contrite over one's sins as to change or decide to change one's ways. To be penitent.

When two people have been separated, it is possible that one of them has behaved in a way that has put the relationship at risk. Reconciliation will depend on that person repenting, being sorry and committed to changing, and the other person forgiving them in return. However, it is also possible that they have both put the relationship at risk by their actions and their reactions. If there is to be reconciliation, then both people will need to be sorry for their behaviour and determined to change and to offer forgiveness to each other.

- *When we forgive someone ... must we always reconcile with them?*

## NO!

When a relationship has been toxic, then to return to it may be unwise and unsafe. It is possible to forgive the toxic person but at the same time accept that your full recovery will depend on you having the courage to distance yourself from them. Reconciliation should only occur when both parties move toward each other with mutual repentance and mutual forgiveness.

- *Does forgiveness mean that justice should not be sought?*

## NO!

Forgiveness is primarily to set *us* free. There are a significant number of forgiven people in jails. All of them have been found guilty of committing a crime and our justice system requires that they serve a time in prison. For every action there is a consequence. When a person drives while under the influence of drugs or alcohol, one consequence might be a fatal accident in which an innocent person dies. If that occurs, a second consequence is that they will most certainly serve a prison sentence. A third consequence might be that the victim's family may choose to live with hatred and bitterness in their hearts, or they may choose to forgive the driver and move on. There is no inconsistency here. Forgiveness does not cancel the process of justice, but justice delivered does not of itself replace the need for forgiveness.

- *Does forgiving another trivialise the wrong done to us?*

## ABSOLUTELY NO!

We have not really understood forgiveness, if by giving it, we are implying that the hurtful event does not matter. The opposite is true. When we do not forgive, it maximises the impact of the wrong done to us.

What has happened does matter, and so does the effect it has had on your life! Those who have hurt us, must be held accountable for the seriousness of their actions.

The circumstances of the event, the event itself, and your response to it have significantly impacted your beliefs, feelings, and behaviour towards others. Whilst forgiving another does not address what has caused your pain, it has the power to completely change your response to the pain. which is negatively impacting your life.

It is now time to revisit our definition:

*'I forgive another, when I set them free from the obligation to suffer at my hands, for the harm they have done to me, as Jesus Christ has set me free from the obligation to suffer for the wrongs I have committed against Him; living thereafter, in the freedom from resentment that only forgiveness can give me.'*

This definition raises one more critical question.

- Is it reasonable to expect that the one who has unjustly hurt us, should pay some price to us for what they have done?

## YES!

But now ask yourself:

- *Who has paid the greatest price so far?*
    - *Is it really the person who has harmed you?*
    - *Or is it yourself?*
- *Has your bitterness or anger punished the perpetrator in your life, to the extent that you are satisfied that the punishment fits the wrong done to you by them?*
- *Or has your bitterness and anger robbed you of the joy and peace you could have enjoyed, with the added consequence of hurting those people who love you?*

Each of these are important questions to be asked, however, it is unlikely that those holding bitterness and resentment toward another, have ever legally or morally punished the person with whom they are justifiably angry. But it is almost guaranteed that they have hurt themselves and those who love them. The impact has been significant and can often be measured by outcomes such as relational breakdowns, social isolation, depression, and mental and physical health issues.

- *Is forgiving someone for offending us, the same process as forgiving someone for a life changing incident like sexual abuse or domestic violence?*

**NO!**

Being offended by another person only hurts us as much as we allow it to. On the other hand, the trauma of abuse or violence is frequently responsible for long lasting mental, physical and relational damage that not only changes the life of the immediate victim ... but the lives of numerous others. Forgiving someone who has *offended* us, involves releasing the person from the obligation of suffering at our hands for what they said or did. Forgiving the person who has *abused* or *violated* us or a family member, involves *much more*. The next few chapters of this book will explore what the *'much more'* is.

## FOR FUTHER REFLECTION

This chapter addressed some of the many questions people have asked us. Consider the ones you or someone close to you are currently asking. As you reflect on our answers, we encourage you to seek out someone who can help you work through any difficulties they might raise for you.

## Chapter Nine

# Three Things …

# THREE THINGS TO DO BEFORE YOU SAY, "I FORGIVE YOU."

#1. "Identify what the hurter *is* and *is not* responsible for.

Our experience in counselling others is that there is often some serious work that needs to be done before we reach the point of forgiving the person we are angry with. In fact, there are three important steps to be taken by the potential forgiver.

The first step is taken when we answer the question, **"What is my hurter responsible and not responsible for?**

In answering this question, it is always important to relive the story. This means telling it to someone who is committed to helping you find the freedom you seek. Now this may be difficult, but it is very helpful. When we have listened to adult survivors of childhood sexual abuse tell their stories, we have seen them discover three things they had not expected:

a) The perpetrator deliberately groomed them with the purpose of sexual gratification in mind, whilst at the same time knowing what they were doing was a criminal act.
b) The perpetrator knew that the person they were abusing was an innocent child.
c) That by swearing the child to secrecy, the perpetrator

was implying that the child was in some way responsible for what was done to them by the abuser.

These three realisations are the truth about what happened and are the real reasons a survivor has for being angry, hurt, and ashamed. None of the blame belongs to the survivor, so if they have mistakenly worn the shame and the guilt, then now is the time to shift it all back to their abuser.

This is the first important step towards freedom from the bitterness and resentment that is destroying their lives. Nothing they did caused the abuse to happen. Even if the perpetrator convinced them that he or she loved them, they as children were innocent of any wrongdoing.

This step is important for anyone, in any circumstance where a person has been overpowered, controlled, or manipulated in a way that leaves them carrying guilt and shame that clearly belong to the perpetrator — not to them.

It is equally relevant for the survivors of domestic violence and workplace or schoolyard bullying. It also applies to adults who, as children, have been victims of continual criticism and verbal abuse from significant others. This step involves embracing the truth of the facts instead of the lies we have been told and believed.

# 2. Accept the responsibility for our response to the event.

Equally important as shifting the blame for the event from us ... to the person who wronged us; is the act of taking responsibility for our responses to the event.

The reason for this is crystal-clear. We cannot pretend that the event did not happen, but we *can* accept that the anger, anxiety and shame we carry is *ours*— and that we have the power to make the choices that will change those painful responses to positive ones.

One helpful way to do this is to think about the people we have hurt ... because of our behaviours that are influenced by the internalised emotions we have chosen to carry. When we take out our anger on someone we love, who is responsible for that outburst ... them or us? The answer is obvious. The anger is ours. It neither belongs to *them* nor to the person who hurt us in the past.

Accepting responsibility for our emotional reactions and the hurtful behaviours that flow from them, involves apologising to those we have hurt and asking for their forgiveness; and in some cases, asking God for his forgiveness also. Let us be very clear ... we are not talking about hurt afflicted on us by another person ... but the hurt we have caused others because we have chosen to internalise bitterness and resentment toward the one who hurt us in the past.

# # 3. Seek to understand what Forgiveness is.

Corrie ten Boom with her father, Casper and sister Betsy lived in the Netherlands during World War 2, and were involved in protecting gypsies and Jews from the Nazis.

They were eventually arrested and after Casper died,

the women were moved to a prison camp called Ravensbrück in Germany. Betsy's health deteriorated quickly but despite the inhumane treatment they received at the hands of the guards, Betsy encouraged Corrie not to be angry but to forgive.

Each night they would read the scriptures which encouraged them to be thankful and forgiving. After Betsy's death, Corrie was released and eventually wrote a book called "The Hiding Place".

She began to travel, preaching at many churches. On one occasion she spoke at a church in Germany and after the service she was approached by a man who had been her guard at Ravensbrück. He had become a Christian and deeply regretted the terrible things he had done. He asked Corrie for forgiveness and held out his hand to her. She did not feel forgiving — yet she asked God to help her as she took his hand. As she did, she began to feel a healing emotion — it was forgiveness.

She writes about what happened next, *"I forgive you brother!" I cried with all my heart. For a long time we held each other's hand — the former guard and the former prisoner. I had never known God's love as deeply as I did then."* Later she wrote, *"Forgiveness, is the key that unlocks the door of resentment and the handcuffs of hatred. It is a power that breaks the chains of bitterness and the shackles of selfishness.* (Corrie ten Boom, 'The Hiding Place')

Nelson Mandela, who was imprisoned for 27 years for protesting against Apartheid, made a life-changing decision the day he was released from prison. *"As I walked out the door and toward the gate that would lead to my freedom, I knew that if I did not leave my bitterness and hatred behind, I'd still be in prison."*

Lewis Smedes, author of 'Forgive and Forget: Healing the Hurts We Don't Deserve,' makes the following statement: *'When we forgive evil, we do not excuse it, we do not tolerate it, we do not smother it. We look evil full in the face, call it for what it is, let its horror shock and stun and enrage us, and only then do we forgive."*

Jesus Christ lived on earth for 33 years. During His entire public ministry, he preached about the love and mercy of God, healed the sick, cleansed the lepers and raised the dead, and commanded His disciples to love their enemies and each other. As he died a cruel death on a cross, He prayed, *"Father, forgive them, for they do not know what they are doing."* For Jesus, offering forgiveness to those who had rejected and crucified Him, was the very reason for which He came to earth.

## WHAT THE BIBLE TEACHES ABOUT FORGIVENESS

The first of the two primary themes of the entire biblical narrative is humanity's **estrangement** from God, and the second is God seeking to facilitate **reconciliation** between Himself and us. Therefore, it follows that the third primary theme is **forgiveness**. For that reason, the Bible teaches extensively through song, story, teaching and parables, precisely what God wants us to know about *separation*, *forgiveness* and *reconciliation*.

In Genesis 37, we meet Joseph who is the second youngest of Jacob's twelve sons. He was his father's favourite son and for that reason was hated by his older brothers. Their hatred of him was made more intense by the fact that he had prophetic dreams, some of which suggested that one day they would serve him. Their anger grew to the point where most of them wanted to kill him. His brother Rueben, however, convinced them not to murder him, but to sell him to Egyptian slave traders and to tell their father that he had been killed by wild animals.

In an amazing way, God protected Joseph over the ensuing years, and eventually — through his ability to interpret dreams — attracted the attention of the Pharoah who was troubled by a dream he did not understand. Joseph interpreted his dream as a divine warning of an upcoming drought. First, there would be seven years of prosperity and then a seven-year drought. Joseph urged Pharoah to appoint someone to lead a project whereby barns would be stocked over the seven good years, so that there would be provision during the seven famine years.

Then came the twist which totally changed Joseph's life. He was appointed to the role of overseer for this project, and in doing so, became the second most powerful person in all of Egypt.

In Genesis Chapter 42, we learn that Jacob, who believed his son Joseph was dead, sent ten of his sons to Egypt to buy grain. Joseph initially concealed his identity, but later revealed, *"I am your brother!" Don't be angry with yourselves or afraid of me. You were not the architects of what happened to me, God was. What you intended for harm has been utilized for good by God, resulting in the preservation of thousands of lives."* This story is just one of many told around these three central themes of the Bible.

Jesus told the parable of the prodigal son. As a young man he demanded that his father give him his inheritance. The demand was tantamount to him saying *"Father, I wish you were dead!"*

Having got what he demanded, he then wasted his inheritance. When he reached the point where he was begging for food and shelter, he remembered that his father's servants had more than enough food to eat. He decided to return home. To his amazement, after all this time his father was still watching the road for his return. When he saw him, he ran to meet him, hugged and kissed him, sobbing, "My son was lost and now he is found."

When Jesus taught the disciples to pray, He taught them to say, 'and forgive us our trespasses as we forgive those who trespass against us'.

He taught Peter that he was to forgive his brother 490 times or in other words, as frequently as necessary. And while on the cross, He forgave those who crucified Him.

When the Apostle Paul was instructing the Colossian Christians on harmonious living, he advised them: *"Since God chose you to be the holy people He loves, you must clothe yourselves with tender-hearted mercy, kindness, humility, gentleness and patience. Make allowance for each other's faults and forgive anyone who offends you. Remember the*

*Lord forgave you, so you must forgive others."*

(Colossians 3:12-13)

The Bible indicates that forgiveness from God is prompted by His grace and love, and reconciliation to Him depends on the individual's willingness to repent for their wrongdoing. A powerful truth is that for us — true forgiveness and reconciliation must be the same.

Appreciation for the divine love and forgiveness we have received, enables us to extend forgiveness to others in a similar manner. The same sense of gratitude encourages and allows us to acknowledge mistakes and make the changes necessary for reconciliation.

The Bible is clear: *to forgive is a choice the hurt person must make ... based on love and grace. To reconcile or not reconcile is also their choice ... based on the true repentance of the hurter.*

# FOR FUTHER REFLECTION

These three steps toward a readiness to forgive, are very important for us to understand and embrace.

- Knowing that the perpetrator is responsible for his/her hurtful behaviour enables us to deal with our false guilt and shame.
- Accepting that we are responsible for our choice to harbour bitterness and resentment means that we also have the power to reverse that choice.
- Understanding what true forgiveness is ... and is not. Embracing it as the way to freedom and healing, serves as the most compelling reason to continue reading this book.

Chapter Ten

# Before You Say ...

# HOW DO I FORGIVE SOMEONE I RESENT?

## a) *Establish a healthy mindset*

Before embarking on the forgiveness journey, it is important to consider your mindset. Check it against the primary reason why you might forgive the person you have been unforgiving and resentful toward. The perpetrator is responsible for their hurtful actions, but not for the resentment that has affected your life since. *We are always responsible for the choice to remain angry and bitter, regardless of how justified it may seem.* Forgiving them as God in Christ has forgiven me, is the only way by which I can break out of the prison that unfortunately my choice has locked me into.

On the other hand, the following statements **should not** be what move us to forgive the one who hurt us.

1. "What they did to me doesn't really matter."
2. "They deserve to be forgiven."
3. "I had no right to be angry at them in the first place."
4. "I probably did something to cause them to hurt me as they did."

### No*!*

Forgiveness must come from a deeper place.

*Your decision to forgive the person who hurt you, is to address the consequences of living with internalised pain.*

Cyril's story was featured in our previous book, 'Walking in the Light at Midnight.' We believe it is important to share it here also.

'I (Graeme) once had a client named Cyril (not his real name). Cyril was referred to me because he had an anger problem. As he marched into my office, he loudly declared that he didn't want to be there. He was sent by someone else. Knowing that I was a pastor as well as a counsellor he further declared that he did not want any 'religious stuff'. I assured him that I did not regard myself as religious and I think that confused him a little. To his credit he spent the next hour honestly describing his anger problem, while all the time blaming his father for it.

'After listening to his story of a lifetime of seeking revenge for what his father had done to him, I asked him a specific question. *"In the present, who has paid the price for your anger about something in your past?"* To my surprise he understood my question, and with tears in his eyes, he named his mother, his wife and his two daughters. He told me that all of them had suffered because of his anger.

'I asked him, as a first step what he was prepared to do now that he had owned the truth that he had hurt them. He said that he was going to ask them to forgive him. I worried all week about what he might do if they refused to do as he asked. When the day came for his second appointment, it was a very different man who walked into my office. His mood was serious, and his demeanour was humble.

'I asked him how it had gone with his confession to his family and his answer bowled me over. He said that three out of the four women had forgiven him willingly. The fourth one, like the others was grateful for his confession but said she would need more time before she could forgive him. Then he added, "I understand that it might take her some time to offer me her forgiveness. Afterall, it has taken me thirty years to forgive my father."

'There were tears in both our eyes as I asked him what he meant. He told me that the experience of being forgiven by three people he loved so dearly, and the joy his mother and his wife and one of his daughters experienced because of their forgiveness of him, motivated him to forgive his father.

'As he was leaving that day, he asked, "Where do you get that sort of psychology from?" Trying to not sound too apologetic I told him I get it from the Bible, to which he responded with a string of expletives as he hugged me, made his next appointment and said goodbye.

'In the sessions that followed, he made it clear that he understood that the price he had been demanding his father pay, as well as the terrible price that the people he loved most in the world, were forced to pay; had already been paid some 2000 years ago by Jesus Christ. And it was because of that gift of love ... he could forgive his father, and his loved ones in turn ... could forgive him.

'Upon reflection, I did nothing, except help him challenge his old mindset. Discovering and embracing the truth made what happened possible.'

b) *Focus on the truth that your reason for forgiving ... is that at last ... you will be released from your prison of internalised pain.*

Forgiveness can be extremely difficult. The person you are being asked to forgive may be an extremely evil person who has sexually abused you and many others.

On the other hand, it may be the former girlfriend who stole your boyfriend and humiliated you in the process. Or it may be the violent marriage partner who battered you with his fists or harangued you with her cruel tongue. Or it might be the friend who used your character references and won your dream job ahead of you.

Although each of these examples are radically different, the hurtful elements are the same. Broken trust, acts of betrayal, deep disappointment, shattered dreams and personal humiliation. Each of these are present in every situation and can be summed up in the words, *"I will never, forgive him or her!"*

Because it is so difficult to forgive, you must keep your mind fixed on why you have come to the point of even considering it as a thing you would do.

If it is true that you are sick of the endless triggers that ignite those outbursts of anger and rage. Or that too often plunge you into those melancholic moods and the deep pits of depression ...

If you no longer want to damage otherwise good friendships with your cynicism, sarcasm and criticism ...

If you hate the loneliness of self-afflicted social isolation and emotional withdrawal ...

*then it is time to change!*

If the brave decision to forgive the person who hurt you, and to forgive yourself, for making the choice to live in this dark prison, is the only way to break free ...

*then, with God's help, that is what you should do!*

c) *Consider what your life and relationships might potentially be like ... if you escaped your prison of internalised emotions.*

You have spent a long time attempting to be both the judge and the hangman — as well as the victim. It has been both exhausting and fruitless. It has not moved you forward to a satisfactory conclusion. You have found yourself in the unwanted position of *victim cum persecutor.*

People who love you have become the unfortunate, albeit unintended targets of your impatience, irritability, outbursts of rage, criticism and sarcasm. If it has not already happened ... you may in the future lose friendships, destroy family relationships and even damage your emotional and physical health.

All of this ... *is not* ... the consequence of being hurt.

It *is* the result of your choice to remain unforgiving.

It is possible that you can alter the course of your current circumstances or future events ... by proceeding with the next step in this process.

**Here you are ...
ready to forgive the person who hurt you.**

# FOR FUTHER REFLECTION

This chapter has focussed on the importance of challenging what you have always thought about forgiveness.

The key question now to consider is this:

What is *the real reason* that I might choose to forgive someone I have been resentful toward?

Chapter Eleven

# How to Turn the Key

# THE KEY TOWARDS FORGIVENESS

𝐴s we begin to understand the actual act of forgiveness, we want you to consider the steps that our friend Alex took. He was conflicted by intense emotional pain, anger and hatred toward his father. At the same time, he had a desire to be obedient to the Holy Spirit's prompting to forgive his father. Eventually he discovered God's model of forgiveness.

Here is Alex's story.

*"When I was a 16 year-old student at Dandenong TAFE, I was bullied by two mature age students. The bullying commenced with small off-the-cuff comments but quickly escalated.*

*"Then after a while, they began sending me explicit on-line material of a homosexual nature, and eventually I was targeted in the bathrooms where they molested me. A common theme throughout all this abuse was my tormentors telling me that 'I deserved it all', and that I 'wanted it'. For some reason, I believed both these messages, which lowered by self-esteem more than it already was.*

*"One evening, I was in the kitchen with my mother, and she asked me about my day. I broke down and confessed everything that had been happening to me. My dad heard the commotion, and I told him as well. He flipped! The first thing he said to me was 'this would never have happened if you had stood up for yourself!'*

*"I didn't know it at the time, but that single sentence had an incredibly negative impact on me over the next few years of my life. I would stew over those words late at night. My already poor mental health and thoughts of inferiority compared to my 'golden-child' big sister, became even more of a problem. I felt that I wasn't the son my dad had wanted.*

*"Every time I failed at something, I felt less and less of a man. I chased after girls, because I thought ... if I had a beautiful girl by my side that I would be seen as enough. I struggled with pornography and ended up sleeping with two of the girlfriends I'd had prior to meeting the young lady who became my wife. I became suicidal and would have regular panic attacks, which came on me suddenly, without warning.*

*"My bitterness toward my dad grew more intense, and we typically kept our distance from each other. When we did engage in conversation it would usually become a yelling match.*

*"As a twenty-year-old, my girlfriend at the time, encouraged me to speak to her about what had happened. I told the story in detail and had no issues recounting what had happened to me, until I got to the part about what my dad had said. I broke down and cried angry tears. I decided then that I would speak to my father about how deeply he had hurt me.*

*"I was quite confrontational in my manner and accusatory in my tone ... as I began telling him how he'd messed up my life. He stood by what he had said*

*to me previously. We yelled at each other, and we even got physical with each other. I told him that I would call the police if he touched me again, then stormed out of the house. I slept at my girlfriend's house for a few days before my mother begged me to return home.*

*"The next couple of years for me were full of anger, bitterness and depression. During this short space of time ... I transferred university degrees ... was made redundant at my place of employment as an engineering technician ... and went through a messy relational breakup.*

*"At age 23, I began a relationship with the lady who would later become my wife. We both had a lot of unresolved baggage to work through. At church, I felt that I was always responding to altar calls, seeking a breakthrough that never came. As a young worship leader, I would always cry and worship from a place of brokenness and pain, and rarely from a place of confidence and joy.*

*"My best friend asked me to do the 'Valiant Man Course' with him. I thought it would be helpful preparation for marriage, so I agreed to go with him. One of the sessions was on forgiveness. I felt the Holy Spirit convict me like never before and I felt him saying, 'You hate your father. All you want is for him to ask for forgiveness, but you refuse to ask for **his** forgiveness for your hatred for him.'*

*"When I got home that night I made a beeline for my parents' room. My father was just getting ready for bed.*

*I said to him, "Dad, I've hated you for a very long time ... can you please forgive me?"*

"That night I saw a snapshot of the heart of my heavenly Father — when, with tears in his eyes, my earthly father said, "Son, I forgave you a long time ago." We embraced, and to my surprise, he asked for my forgiveness as well.

"I am now 32 years old, and it's ten years since I forgave my dad. Since that time, I have seen God continue to work on both me, my dad and our relationship. He is one of my best friends. One of the happiest memories I have is the moment I told him I was going to be a father myself.

"As never before, I appreciated the impact certain traumatic events had on my father's life. His father had died when he was three years old. He was regularly beaten by his older brother, who was 20 years older than him — yet the closest thing to a father figure he had in his childhood. In addition to this, growing up in communist Romania had hardened my father in many ways I could not comprehend.

"Through the restorative grace and power of God, miraculously I began to understand that my fathers' hurtful comment so many years ago, was said more from the perspective of, "I have failed as a father," in terms of preparing me for life — rather than my failure as a son. I have seen my father's heart soften, and a tenderness come out of him that I did not think existed.

*I finish my story with a quote I came across, which resonates with me:*

*'I try to love my dad for who he is ... and forgive him for who he isn't.'* "

## HELPFUL STEPS TO FORGIVING ANOTHER.

STEP 1. Revisit the painful event

In the field of Psychology, this concept may occasionally, be mistaken for 'therapeutic catharsis', which entails expressing or acting out one's anger and aggression with the objective of lessening its impact. What we are recommending, however, is to tell your story and give yourself the opportunity to explore your feelings at the time of the event ... to recognise what you did with them then ... how they impact you now.

This is exactly what Alex did. Even when forgiving his father was not high on his priority list, he unwittingly took the first step toward forgiveness — he told his story. And in doing so, he revisited the most painful event in his life, in the presence of someone else. This step can be an extremely difficult thing to do.

During the time I (Graeme), was counselling at the Elkanah Christian Community in Marysville — a lady whom we will call Linda — made an appointment to visit me for counselling. She had driven over 100kms to get there for a one-hour appointment.

When I invited her to tell me her story, she was unable to speak. Was it the pain of the abuse or the fear of reconnecting with the terrible shame she felt about having been abused? It may well have been either or both.

We sat together in silence for an hour, then she left. After arriving home, she rang the office to make another appointment, commenting to the secretary that she had found the session very helpful. This happened four weeks in a row before she could actually speak.

The story Linda eventually told me happened to be one of the most harrowing I had ever heard. Yet as she told it, it was as if it had happened yesterday, but somehow she began to comprehend things that she had never understood. She realised for the first time that the man who had abused her as a little girl, knew that what he was doing was a crime, and yet he had patiently groomed her for the sexual encounters that had so damaged her.

For the first time she could call him a paedophile, and understand and accept that *he* — not herself — was to blame for her abuse. The shame she had carried most of her life was his, *not hers*. Her sobbing and tears expressed the anger she had carried for so long, but never understood. For the first time also, she felt the pain of broken trust. This would not be the last time in her counselling sessions that she would revisit aspects of her childhood, but each time she did ... it brought new revelations of the hope for healing that was now hers.

As we said earlier, one of the benefits that comes from revisiting a painful event is that we learn to differentiate between what is the truth and what is not. Linda had always thought of her abuser as a good man who did what he did to her because she was a bad girl. She now acknowledged him as an evil person who felt and thought nothing for her at all.

On the other hand, Alex, who had also thought so poorly of himself, was consumed with hatred for his father, which he had expressed when he first confronted him.

When challenged by God — as we all are — to forgive those we are at angry at, Alex already knew what he should do. He had already recognised that his poor mental health and his bitterness was not only a result of the words his father had spoken over him, but also the hatefulness he held in his heart. The only remedy for him to heal from his inner pain, was to forgive his father and to be forgiven by him.

## STEP 2. Seek forgiveness from others and God.

Before you attempt to forgive the person who hurt you ... take the time to ask those people whom you may have hurt — even unintentionally — *to forgive you.*

Tell them that you are sorry for your irritability, your anger, your emotional withdrawal, or whatever behaviour you know has affected them. As you do this, you will experience joy and freedom flowing into your life when they forgive you.

Now, ask God to forgive you ... remembering His promise through the Apostle John, "*If we confess our sins, He is faithful and just to forgive us our sins, and to cleanse us from all unrighteousness.*" *(1 John 1:9)*

Did you notice that Alex did not burst into his parents' bedroom and tell his father that he forgave him? No. Instead, he confessed his long-held hatred towards his dad, and asked his father to forgive him. In Alexs' case, it led to reconciliation with his father, and a growing understanding and appreciation of *his own* fathers' life journey.

STEP 3. Forgive the person who has hurt you.

Now — you are ready to forgive! You have been reminded of the power of forgiveness through being forgiven by your friends and family ... and especially by God. Christ has given us a divine example — *"but God demonstrated His love toward us ... in that while we were still sinners ... Christ died for us."* (Romans 5:8)

Furthermore, you are now ready to obey the scriptures which say: *"And forgive one another as God in Christ has forgiven you."* (Ephesians 4:32)

**You *do not* need to *feel forgiving*.**
**You *do* need to *feel grateful*.**

God's forgiveness was offered to us through His grace ... and our forgiveness is offered to others out of gratitude for that grace.

**Feeling forgiving ...**
**will always follow the act of forgiving.**

Remember, whatever forgiving the person who hurt you means to them ... it means so much more to you. You are the one being set free! You are bursting out through the bars of your prison!

## You are taking your life back!

Say the words, "I forgive you."

- Use the person's name.
- Repeat your statement of forgiveness as many times as you need to.
- Remind yourself that you are forgiving them as *God-in-Christ has forgiven you.*

Remember, Jesus has not only died for the sins you have committed against Him and others, but for every wrong that has ever been committed against you by someone else.

### STEP 4. Turn your tombstones into milestones.

This is where you come face-to-face with the truth that you can forgive but you cannot forget. At this point you are anxious about the probability that the memories of the betrayal ... the abuse ... those acts of violence will continue. Those memories have been like tombstones. Whenever they occur, they cause you grief. They are triggers. Perhaps, if they continue you will begin to think that you have not really forgiven the person who hurt you so deeply, after all.

Once upon a time, in our living memory, on country roads in Australia, every mile you travelled would take you past a white stone or small white post, with a number painted on it. It was originally called a milestone — with the number on it, to tell you how far you had come since you passed the last one, and how far you had to go before you reached your destination.

*The good news is that God has the power and the will to transform your tombstones into milestones, and when He does ... every painful memory will become a memorial to your healing, rather than a reminder of your pain.*

The potential is that you can allow God to do that with every *new* disappointment or hurt that you experience in your whole life journey. It is a beautiful thing when God gives you the grace to say:

*"Father, I willingly give you permission to transform every potential tombstone into a milestone. Thank you."*

STEP 5. Pray a forgiveness prayer.

We have often joined people as they have prayed their way to forgiveness, and we thought it might be helpful to share what the common elements of those prayers have been.

## CONFESSION AND REPENTANCE

This is an acknowledgement of the negative impact of non-forgiveness. It often includes confessing to God the intensity of their anger towards the person they need to forgive has been, and how often their feelings and thoughts have been bitter and revengeful.

We have heard people confessing and repenting of the bitterness that has impacted their view of life — the outbursts of anger directed at loved ones, and harsh words spoken to children and partners. Sometimes, their prayers of confession have focussed on particular people whom they have wounded, by internalising the anger and the bitterness they felt toward the person who had hurt them. We have heard people asking God to forgive them for the pain they have caused Him and the people they love. We have heard them pray for the courage to apologise to their loved ones for their hurtful behaviour and to ask them for forgiveness.

## ASKING FOR & ACCEPTING GOD'S FORGIVENESS

Confession and repentance are almost always followed by requesting their Heavenly Father's forgiveness and their acceptance of it. This is often accompanied by expressions of unworthiness and sorrow, followed by a deep sense of joy when they accept the realisation that God in Christ has forgiven them.

For those who are uncertain about how and what to pray, we are including this model prayer below. You can use it as your own prayer or simply as an inspiration for how you want to pray. It sometimes helps to pray in the presence of another person who can also pray forgiveness and healing over your life.

**NOTE:** Leave out whatever is not appropriate and add whatever fits your situation.

> *"Dear Father God. Thank you for loving me even when I feel undeserving and messed up in my mind.*
>
> *You know that ever since ......name the incident(s)......  I have felt hurt, betrayed, wounded, unworthy*

anxious, angry and afraid.

My trust in the people I thought loved me has been broken. I struggle to feel safe in relationships, I have even felt guilty for things I know now I was not responsible for. I have been locked in this prison for a long time.

I now know that I can make the choice to be free.

Lord, You know that I have often projected my anger, anxiety and false guilt onto my family, the people in my workplace, and on myself.
I get angry too often, I drink too much. I have become dependent on medication.

Please forgive me so that I know I am forgiven.

Give me the courage to ask my family members and friends for forgiveness and give me the humility to accept and love those who might find that hard to do.

The Lord Jesus taught us to pray "Forgive us our sins as we forgive those who sin against us."

I have struggled with the thought of forgiving ……name the person…… , but I know that if he/she came to You asking You for forgiveness, You would forgive them in the same way You have forgiven me. I believe that You have not only died for the sins I have committed against you and others; but you have also died for ……name the person……'s sins against me.

*I believe that Lord ... with all my heart.*

*I set ...name the person... free from the obligation to suffer for what they did to me, just as you have set me free from the obligation to suffer for the sin's I have committed against you and others."*

**Pause ... with open hands ... and declare:**

*"Lord, I now receive Your forgiveness ... I receive Your healing and Your peace. Thank you."*

Chapter Twelve

# Be-Attitudes of Forgiveness

# JESUS' WORDS ON LOVE AND FORGIVENESS AND OUR RESPONSE

#1. *"God blesses those who are merciful, for they will be shown mercy." (Matthew 5:7)*

At the commencement of His public ministry, Jesus spoke of eternal truth that clashed with what was being taught by the religious leaders of that time. It still does.

This statement of Jesus does not stand alone. It is one of eight statements that precede His startling description of those who live by the values of the Kingdom — as the 'salt of the earth' and the 'light of the world.'

He tells the crowd that God blesses ... *'those who are poor in spirit, and realise their need for Him ... those who mourn, for they will be comforted ... those who are humble, for they will inherit the earth ... those who hunger and thirst for justice, for they will be satisfied ... those who are merciful, for they will be shown mercy ... those whose hearts are pure, for they will see God ...those who are peace-makers, they will be called the children of God ... and those who are persecuted for doing right, for the Kingdom of Heaven is theirs.'*

The promise that accompanies 'God blesses the merciful' is that *'they shall receive mercy.'* This is a common element of Jesus' teaching on mercy and forgiveness. It's like He is saying:

"Do you want to unlock the treasures of divine mercy and forgiveness? Do you want to stand in awe at the unfathomable depth and unlimited supply of the Father's love and grace? Then be merciful and forgiving. That is the key."

#2. *"You have heard the law that says the punishment must match the injury. An eye for an eye and a tooth for a tooth, but I say, do not resist an evil person. If someone slaps you on the right cheek offer the other cheek also. If you are sued in court and your shirt is taken from you, give your coat too. If a soldier demands you carry his gear for one mile, carry it two miles. Give to those who ask and don't turn away from those who want to borrow."*
(Matthew 5:38-42)

Jesus is speaking here to people who live in an occupied territory. The Roman army — the occupiers — like most occupying nations, were particularly cruel. They sought to dominate and intimidate the citizens of Jerusalem, by tormenting and persecuting them. Jesus was saying that the way of the Kingdom was not to fight back but to seek a way to bless their enemy.

Three years later, He demonstrated exactly what that would look like. Mercilessly tortured by Roman soldiers, He was forced to carry His cross and suffer the pain and humiliation of crucifixion. Then just before He died, He looked out at the soldiers and the crowd who had been shouting insults at Him and cried out, *"Father, forgive them, for they do not know what they are doing."* (Luke 23:34)

In my imagination ... I can see myself there in the crowd, as a quiet observer. Standing there, I am full of wonder at the intensity of the hatred, and the heat of the fervour, which drove the madness that demanded the death of a man who had committed no crime. Then I look at His face. It is contorted by the pain inflicted on Him, and his struggle to breathe. I see His eyes. They are filled with compassion — as instead of protesting His innocence or calling down curses on His enemies, He asks His Father to forgive them!

#3. *"You have heard the law that says, love your neighbour and hate your enemy. But I say, love your enemies. Pray for those who persecute you. In that way you will be acting like your Father in heaven. For he gives His sunlight to both the evil and the good and he sends rain on the just and the unjust alike. If you love only those who love you, what reward is there for that? Even corrupt tax gatherers do that much. If you are kind only to your friends, how are you different from anyone else? Even pagans do that. But you are to be perfect, as your Father in heaven is perfect."*
(Matthew 5:43-48)

In Genesis 3 we read about Adam and Eve making a choice that from then till now ... has impacted the universe. It was the choice to either be content with being *like* God, in His image — or to *be as* God — in His place.

They chose the latter.

Now in the passage above, we hear Jesus telling those who gathered around Him, that if they love their enemies and pray for their persecutors, they will be imitating their Father in Heaven. More than that, they will be like Him. If the term *'corrupt tax gatherers'* indicated a moral low point, then *'loving your enemies'* was the opposite to that. Those who were only kind to their friends were doing what even pagans do — those who had made the same choice as Adam and Eve did. It is unlikely that we will show love and kindness to our enemies ... unless we have made the conscious choice to be like Him.

*#4. "Forgive us our sins as we have forgiven those who have sinned against us."* Matthew 6:12

In the Lord's Prayer, Jesus says *the most* powerful thing about forgiveness. It stands out not only because it's one of the six petitions we are taught to bring before God each time we pray, but also because it alludes to — so early in His ministry — God's redemptive plan. That plan includes the unconditional forgiveness offered to sinners through the death and resurrection of His Son, Jesus Christ.

As one of these six petitions, it is strategically placed between *'give us today, the food we need',* and *'don't let us yield to temptation, but rescue us from the evil one.'* In both these petitions we affirm our dependence on God. In the first one — we are asking for His preserving and nurturing of our lives in a physical sense. And in the second one — we are asking for His protection and deliverance from the evil one who seeks to destroy us spiritually.

If we are to be a people who experience the power and freedom God's forgiveness brings, then we must remember ... it will *always be in proportion to the degree to which we forgive those who sin against us.* Our capacity to forgive others, is something God will provide, as willingly as provision for our bodies and protection and deliverance for our souls.

The discipline we all need to apply to our lives, is to daily exercise our dependence on God for the grace to both receive His forgiveness ... and to pass it on to others.

*#5. "If you forgive those who sin against you, your heavenly Father will forgive you. But if you refuse to forgive others, your Father will not forgive your sins."* (Matthew 6:14-15)

This statement immediately follows the Lord's prayer and seems to be almost a repetition of what the prayer says. However, it is significant for this reason: each of the other petitions in the prayer were included in the forms of worship commonly used in the temple — but not the fifth one. So, what Jesus says provides us with an explanation as to why He included it.

It may have confused His audience, as it seems to make God's forgiveness of us conditional on us forgiving others. There are conditions in the forgiveness process such as *confession* and *repentance*.

It is unlikely that we will offer true forgiveness to someone who has hurt us without first confessing to God that we have sinned by living with anger in our hearts. Jesus puts forgiving others with receiving God's forgiveness as both a promise and a warning, for the very reason that He wants us to always remember the importance of *confession* and *repentance*.

THE PROMISE ...
*He will forgive:*

THE WARNING ...
*if you do not forgive, your Father in Heaven will not forgive you.'*

The qualities that Jesus demonstrated
when he paid the price for our sin were
*love, humility* and *generosity.*
Receiving God's forgiveness
and forgiving others
requires the same qualities in us.

Chapter Thirteen

# Pay Up … Or Else …

# JESUS' WORDS ON LOVE AND FORGIVENESS AND OUR RESPONSE ... continued

*F*ollowing on from the previous chapter, we continue to unpack Jesus' teaching about forgiveness.

#6. "Then Peter came to Jesus and asked, "Lord how often should *I forgive someone* who sins against me? *Seven times?*' '*No, not seven times,*' Jesus replied, '*But seventy times seven!*"

"Therefore, the Kingdom of Heaven can be compared to a King who decided to bring his accounts up to date with servants who had borrowed money from him. In the process, one of his debtors who owed him millions of dollars was brought in. He could not pay, so his master ordered that he be sold, along with his wife, his children and everything he owned — to pay the debt.

"The man fell before his master and begged him, 'Please be patient with me and I will pay it all'. "Then, his master was filled with pity for him, and he released him and forgave his debt. But when the man left the king, he went to a fellow servant who owed him a small debt. He grabbed him by the throat and demanded instant payment.

"His fellow servant fell before him and begged for a little more time. 'Be patient with me, and I will pay it,' he pleaded. But his creditor could not wait. He had his fellow-servant arrested and put in prison until the debt could be fully paid.

"When the other servants saw this, they were upset. They went to the king and told him everything that had happened. Then the king called in the man he had forgiven and said, 'You evil *servant! I forgave you that tremendous debt because you pleaded with me. Shouldn't you have had mercy on your fellow servant, just as I had mercy on you? Then the angry king sent the man to prison, to be tortured until he had paid his entire debt."*

*"That's what my heavenly Father will do to you if you refuse to forgive your brothers and sisters from your heart."*
(Matthew 18:21-35)

Jesus' reply to Peter's question, and the parable he told, must be taken separately. His response to Peter's suggestion — that forgiving someone seven times for the same misbehaviour might be more than enough — was that a more accurate answer would be, 'seventy times seven.' The inference is that if you were still counting when you reached seven, then you had not truly forgiven the person any of the previous times.

The parable is really a commentary on 'forgive us our sins as we forgive those who sin against us,' prompted by Peter's demonstration that he had not yet understood that statement. We might conclude that Jesus has offered nothing new about forgiveness — but we would be wrong.

The key points of the parable are:

### a) The master's willingness to forgive the servant purely out of compassion.

- Every sin we commit is a debt. We are all debtors and are dependent on God for forgiveness.
- We can never pay the debt of sin, so unless we

are forgiven the debt, we remain burdened and under judgement.

- Just as everyone incurs debt, everyone has the potential to benefit from God's unlimited compassion.

b) **The servant's unforgiving and unrelenting attitude to his fellow servant, indicating a complete lack of compassion** (verses 28-30)

- The unforgiving servant, pardoned of his huge debt, refused to forgive his fellow servant a small debt. Jesus is teaching His listeners that the man represents the many believers who refuse to forgive. The fellow servant represents those who may have been forgiven by God for their sins against Him, but not by the believers they have wronged.

- Jesus illustrates here that there is much more involved in unforgiveness than just the desire for justice. This man is angry, ungrateful, violent, proud, arrogant, and revengeful. Jesus also shows that, in human terms, it is possible for a sinner to accept God's transforming forgiveness — and yet still resist being transformed.

c) **One act of unforgiveness may negatively affect many people.** (Verse 31)

In the parable, the fellow servants of the two men were upset. I imagine they have been on a roller coaster of emotions. One of their number is brought before their master, because he owes him a great debt. They are worried for their friend. If he is guilty, he will be jailed and his wife and children will be sold into slavery. Their worry turns to sheer amazement when the normally arrogant servant prostrates himself before his master. Then their amazement turns to joyful astonishment when the master forgives him.

Their joy, however, does not last long. It suddenly turns to unbelief, then sorrow, and finally, anger, when the man returns to his arrogant and prideful self, refusing to forgive a man who owed him a fraction of the debt for which he himself had been forgiven. Motivated by their anger, they approached their master to report what they had observed, fully aware of his how he would respond.

d) **The master's just response to the forgiven man after he refuses to forgive his fellow servant.**

In this parable the servant falls out of favour with his master because of his debt. He was forgiven by the master's compassion. He faces permanent separation because of his refusal to extend forgiveness to his fellow servant.

Jesus is teaching that *our eternal separation* from Him *will never be for our refusal to forgive others*, but for the *pride, arrogance, disobedience, and self-determination* that lies *behind our refusal to accept His forgiveness.*

Jesus was asking his listeners to examine their hearts, and determine whether following Him, and trusting Him as their Saviour and Lord was their unambiguous intention. Following Him would involve imitating Him and that will always include 'forgiving others as He has forgiven us.'

*#7. "I tell you, you can pray for anything, and if you believe that you have received it, it will be yours. But when you are praying, first forgive anyone you are holding a grudge against, so that your Father in heaven will forgive your sins too."*
(Mark 11: 22-25)

The question to be addressed is: *by what means does the Lord Jesus Christ manage, at such a significant cost, to thoroughly forgive us, thereby transforming us into individuals who willingly and wholly forgive those who have wronged us?*

The Apostle John gives us the answer. *"Dear friends, let us continue to love one another, for love comes from God. But anyone who does not love does not know God, for God is love. God showed how much He loved us by sending His one and only Son into the world so that we might have eternal life through Him. This is real love – not that we loved God, but that He loved us and sent His Son as a sacrifice to take away our sin.*

*"Dear friends, since God so loved us that much, we surely ought to love each other. No one has ever seen God. But if we love each other, God lives in us, and His love comes to full expression in us.*

*"God has given us His Spirit as proof that we live in Him and He in us. Furthermore, we have seen with our own eyes and now testify that the Father sent His Son to be the Saviour of the world. All who confess that Jesus is the Son of God, have God living in them, and they live in God. We know how much God loves us, and we have put our trust in His love." God is love, and all who live in love, live in God and God lives in Him."*
(1 John 4: 7-15)

## Claire's Story (Not her real name)

"I was born in England shortly after WW2 ended. My parents, then 49 and 39 were loving, kind and generous — but they sheltered me to a fault. They had not only grown up with the discipline of life in the early 1900s, as children, but also lived through two world wars as adults.

"My Dad was a GP, and he and Mum had been involved in performing operations underground in WW2 London, with bombs exploding above them. I wanted to become a GP like him. He was my hero and Mum was an angel. They were both committed Christians, and I loved attending Church and Sunday School as a child.

"School was a happy place and my results were good. However, at 8 years of age, I joined my older brother Alan at boarding school. I never was an extrovert ... so boarding school was quite daunting for me. Our teachers and matrons all seemed so ancient to me. They were extremely strict. Coming from a Methodist household to a high Anglican Church of England school was a shock. I could not understand the long prayers, spoken in 'ye olde English' and attending church became tedious.

"I left school at 16. My grades were not good and my dream of following my father into medicine had faded. In 1963 I attended Secretarial College, in

London, from which I graduated with honours. My life was about to change. I followed my friends into a whole new lifestyle that did not include going to Church.

"In my second year at Secretarial College, I attended a party and met a married man, who throughout the night plied me with alcohol. The next morning, I woke, lying on my back on a hard floor. I knew what had happened and I was devastated. I blamed myself. It was my fault. I was the guilty party. The shock and shame haunted me for many years.

"Alan travelled to Australia where he became a Jackaroo. When he returned to England for his 21$^{st}$ birthday, he encouraged me to move to Australia. Alan sponsored me and, in 1966 I arrived in Melbourne and immediately started work as a secretary. My parents had both retired, so they decided to join us — arriving in 1967. They bought a house, and I moved in with them. It was great to experience family life again. However, I continued to struggle with my buried guilt and shame.

"About this time, I met a young man called Ross, and told my Mum the next day that I had met the man I was going to marry. We went out together for four tumultuous years. His controlling (psychopathic) nature kept rising to the surface. I was a compliant person who had learnt that disobedience led to painful consequences, so I gave into him all the time. Eventually we married, and I continued to tolerate his tempers, silent treatment, deceit, and financial greed.

*He ruled by fear.*

"When our first son Daniel, arrived on the scene, Ross was not the loving father I had hoped he would be. He abused Daniel from an early age. I tried to stop him, but he was stronger than I, and his shocking temper was frightening. Because of this I did not want a second child, but in a rare peaceful moment I was persuaded otherwise. Two years later Paul was born.

"Daniel had a strong personality like his father. Paul, like me, preferred to talk things through and disliked arguments. The atmosphere in our home was often explosive especially when Daniel became a teenager. None of us knew when or why Ross's next outburst would happen.

Ross commenced a business from our home in which I worked for him for four years. The only time I got to go out was when we attended Rotary functions where Ross played the part of the loving family man and husband.

"Daniel started running away from home when he was fourteen — I was heartbroken and paralysed with fear. Ross disowned our son and forbade me to see him. The only time I was able to see Daniel was when I was away from home, and without my husband's knowledge. I perpetually walked on eggshells.

"In 1989 Ross left us, announcing that he was moving interstate for three years after which we would reunite. I knew that we would never reunite, and his words were a great relief.

"The day he left, Paul and I hugged each other in gratitude for his departure. No more fearful anticipation of the next explosion. We could relax. Daniel returned to live with us, but living with a drug addict was a strain I could not endure for long.

"I divorced Ross in 1992 and felt a massive sense of relief. Whilst he had scarred Daniel and Paul over many years, he could never hurt us again. Paul and I have a remarkably close bond, but Daniel still wears the scars and lives alone.

"Paul made decision to become a Christian through a Schoolteacher, as he realised he needed God's guidance in his life. Over the years, God has helped him through many challenging times. The Lord used Paul to lead me back to Him ... and in 2002, I was baptised.

"I have since conquered my fear and my guilt, and finally have forgiven myself and others who have wronged me. I still am not an extrovert, but I have courage and am empathetic with those who struggle — having helped several friends. I am eternally grateful to God for turning my life around.

"Being part of God's family is especially important to me. Paul is still the most wonderful son and friend a mother could have. God had a plan, and He is awesome."

Having read Claire's story ... can you see? We have not only been *pardoned* but we also have a *new address!* We no longer live in a place where it is natural and acceptable to hate our enemies, or to live with anger and resentment toward those who hurt us. Nor is it acceptable to engage in self-hatred and to continue living with shame and guilt.

We have moved to a new neighbourhood.

We now live in God and He lives in us ... and consequently we now love others as He loves us.

*"Such love has no fear because perfect love casts out all fear. If we are afraid, it is for fear of punishment, and this shows that we have not fully experienced His perfect love. We love each other because He loved us first."* (1 John 4:18)

At our new address, Jesus is our **Landlord** and our **Banker** as well as **Mayor** of the city. He loves us with perfect love. He paid our removal costs, and He waives our rent. He has granted us permanent residency and has signed an unbreakable contract. He demonstrates His love to us through His unlimited patience and kindness. He is good and faithful and always gentle. And He has given us His Holy Spirit so that we can be like Him.

We are now capable of loving others and ourselves ... just as He loves us. And the bonus is ... that we get the opportunity to demonstrate that love ... by being peaceful and forgiving toward others.

Chapter Fourteen

# The Final Word on Forgiveness

# THE FINAL WORD

In this book, we have taken tried and tested psychological understandings and principles and combined them with equally tried and tested truths and directives from the Bible. Together, they form a powerful, working model of forgiveness. This model has the potential to liberate us from prisons of bitterness, anger and shame ... and many other negative and painful emotions. In the interests of clarity and application, for this final chapter, we will attempt to summarize them as simply as possible.

### Principle 1:

The most destructive effect of a traumatising event is rarely, if ever, the event itself. The longest lasting and most damaging impact comes in the form of one or two emotional responses.

The first ... is the internalising of painful emotions like fear, anger and guilt. The common consequences of such internalisation are fits of rage, seeking revenge, social withdrawal and the inability to build and maintain healthy relationships.

The second most common emotional response ... is a false guilt and shame which leads to extreme self-loathing, self-effacement, and self-punishment. These responses frequently lead to addictive behaviours, depression, anxiety and psychiatric conditions.

### Principle 2:

Most people believe that justice should be dealt to the person who has wronged us, but it is rarely enough.

Holding on to anger and resentment is the result of a false belief that it somehow punishes the one who hurt us. Of course this is not the truth. However, the truth is ... that holding on to these painful emotions actually hurts us emotionally, physically, psychologically and relationally.

### Principle 3:

Forgiveness is not given for the benefit of the 'wounder' but for the benefit of the 'wounded'.

The reality is that the importance of forgiveness is that it is the only effective way to release ourselves from the negative impact of remaining bitter and resentful. It does not specifically address the hurtful consequences of the event, nor does it eliminate the painful memories. It does, however, start us on a journey where the behaviours of others do not automatically plunge us into long term resentment.

### Principle 4:

Experiencing God's unlimited and unconditional forgiveness empowers us to forgive others in the same way.

The freedom that comes to those who — by faith — know that God has forgiven us from the wrongs we have committed against Him, is life changing and transformational. This freedom comes with the command and empowerment to pay it forward.

### Principle 5:

Jesus has not only died for every wrong we have committed but for every wrong that has ever been committed against us.

> *'Since God chose you to be the holy people He loves, you must clothe yourselves with tender hearted mercy, kindness, humility, gentleness and patience.*
>
> *Make allowance for each other's faults and forgive anyone who offends you. Remember, the Lord forgave you, so you must forgive others.*
>
> *Above all, clothe yourselves with love, which binds us together in perfect harmony. And let the peace that comes from Christ, rule in your hearts.*
>
> *For as members of one body, you are called to live in peace. And always be thankful.'*
>
> *(Colossians 3: 12-15)*